201 KILLER COVER LETTERS

201 KILLER COVER LETTERS

THIRD EDITION

Sandra Podesta & Andrea Paxton

Mc
Graw
Hill
Education

New York   Chicago   San Francisco   Athens   London   Madrid
Mexico City   Milan   New Delhi   Singapore   Sydney   Toronto

3 4 5 6 7 8 9 0   QFR/QFR   1 0 9 8 7 6 5 4

ISBN 978-0-07-183157-4
MHID 0-07-183157-6

e-ISBN 978-0-07-183158-1
e-MHID 0-07-183158-4

Library of Congress Cataloging-in-Publication Data
Podesta, Sandra.
  201 killer cover letters / Sandra Podesta and Andrea Paxton. — Third edition.
    pages cm
  ISBN 978-0-07-183157-4 (pbk.)
  ISBN 0-07-183157-6 (pbk.)
  1. Cover letters. 2. Applications for positions. 3. Job hunting. I. Paxton, Andrea.
II. Paxton, Andrea. III. Title. IV. Title: Two hundred and one killer cover letters.
V. Title: Two hundred one killer cover letters.
  HF5383.P63 2014
  650.14'2—dc23
                                                2013041730

Contents

Introduction

SINCE THE FIRST and second editions of our book were published, the world has changed in dramatic ways, many of which have affected the job market and the job search process. The greatest change in the job hunt is that it now takes place almost entirely online. Thanks to the Internet, you can identify your preferred geographic location, industry, organization, and position without leaving your desk. You can network, apply, and even interview online.

In many profound ways, the Internet makes the search far easier. It's equally easy, however, to be lulled into a false complacency that can significantly extend the length of your search and compromise your success. For example, the incredible simplicity of applying for jobs online means that many people apply for jobs they are unqualified to fill, which can swell an applicant pool to an unwieldy size. As a result, truly qualified applicants can be overlooked. To get noticed, to make a genuine impact, the serious candidate has to work harder and smarter, networking more effectively and making contact more strategically *and more frequently* than ever before.

Do you hate to write? Most people do. But this book makes it easy! And here's why your cover letters are so vital to your success: employers don't want to hire a list of jobs, job responsibilities, dates, degrees, coursework, and affiliations. They want to hire a *person*—a living, breathing human being. Someone with a personality. A humorous coworker or a serious one. A team player or a self-starter. An intuitive thinker or someone who takes direction well. Sure, they want to hire a candidate with the appropriate skills, but they've got to like that person (*you*), too.

After all, they'll be working with you on a daily basis—and the better everyone gets along, the more productive the work will be.

What this means is that you must project your personality, or some aspect of it, from the very first ad you respond to and in the very first letter you write. The reason is that, to make a hiring decision, your next employer is looking for the answers to four vital questions:

1. Do you have the skills that this job requires?
2. Will you be compatible with my team?
3. Are you honest and willing to work, and do you have the right attitude?
4. Are you a good fit for my organization?

Your resume will answer the first question. Your letters or e-mails, interviews, and references will answer the other three questions. Thus, your jobhunting letters are an essential opportunity to make yourself stand out as a unique and interesting person, someone who an employer would like to meet, interview, hire, and work beside.

To get an edge over your competition, you should not only write, but write often. Why? Most job applicants—your competition—never follow up after an interview. Of those who do, many write letters that are so inadequate that they actually impair what might have been a perfectly acceptable candidacy. Furthermore, most job search letters are forgotten after a quick review. What this means is that writing your potential employer at all can put you ahead of other candidates. Writing a strong, impressive letter can put you miles ahead. And writing frequently can give you what advertisers call "top-of-mind awareness": it can keep you on your next employer's "radar" no matter how long the hiring decision takes.

Don't despair, there is good news! Writing effectively is not as hard as you think. You don't have to be a Pulitzer Prize–winning journalist. You don't have to use eight four-syllable words per paragraph. You don't have to make your correspondence any longer than it needs to be; writing voluminous letters won't guarantee that you'll get hired. You only have to make yourself understood. You need to know what you want to say, and you need to say it clearly, accurately, and concisely.

And that is precisely what this book will help you achieve. With this book, and the downloadable content that accompanies it, you hold in your hands a powerful advantage. Because the vast majority of jobhunters will choose not to write cover letters or e-mails, when you do, you will stand out from your competition in an important way. Suddenly, you will get noticed as the one who is thorough, takes the extra step, is not lazy, and strives for what he or she wants. In short, *you* will be the person who appeals to your next employer as being precisely the representative who will contribute to the success of his or her organization. And that is what it takes to land the job you want.

This book is the product of our successful jobhunting seminar, and of years of work in recruiting, writing resumes, branding, and marketing communications. Our clients use our techniques and achieve results. They are selected for interviews more often and offered the positions they are after. Frequently, we hear that a major benefit our seminar delivered was the simple encouragement to try something different in a letter. Openings that intrigue. Body copy that boasts. Formats that fascinate. We're delighted! We hope this book will do the same for you.

Acknowledgments

WE ARE GRATEFUL to you, our readers, who trust us for support in making your searches more effective, more quickly. By crafting and using killer cover letters, not only are you adopting a proactive approach to the search process, but you are sparking more interest in your qualifications, attracting more potential employers with whom to interview, and increasing the speed with which you land the job you want. We are gratified when our advice proves integral to your jobhunting success. We wish you a speedy search and a successful career!

Sandra Podesta
Andrea Paxton

How to Use This Book

and the Accompanying Downloadable Content

201 KILLER COVER Letters is for any job seeker who finds it difficult to write the perfect cover letter—and that's almost all of us! This book tells you how to write every type of job search letter you'll ever need and puts at your fingertips a library of letters that will get noticed and get results.

> *Please note that throughout this book, the word* letter *refers to any and all types of written communication, including e-mail, handwritten notes, and even typed letters sent via "snail mail."*

The special bonus downloadable content contains all 201 killer cover letters featured in the book. You don't even have to retype them—just change the specifics to suit your circumstances, and they're ready to send!

Before using the downloadable content, peruse the book. If you're pressed for time, at least read Chapters 1 and 2, which provide information on jobhunting online, as well as the basic dos and don'ts for writing effective job search letters. Chapter 3 helps you identify and position your strengths. Take a few minutes to complete Worksheets 3-1, 3-2, and 3-3 in this chapter. Doing so will furnish you with several powerful sentences that you can use immediately in the body copy of your letters.

Then you can move on to the specific chapters that focus on the particular type of letter you're writing; in each chapter, you'll find sample letters, as well as a choice of sample openings and closings. (Every letter is numbered; Letter 5-12, for example, refers to Chapter 5, Letter 12.) The title of each letter gives the industry or the specific position that is of interest to the job seeker, and in some cases mentions issues that are addressed in the letter. For example, a heading that includes "Job Loss" indicates that the letter contains a reference to downsizing, layoffs, a job being eliminated, a merger or acquisition, the challenging economy, or another such scenario that affects either the writer or the reader. "Workforce Return" demonstrates that the letter is from someone who is returning to the job market after time away. "Salary" indicates a salary discussion that may provide ideas for you to use. "Confidentiality" refers to a request for discretion in contacting the jobhunter at his or her present place of employment, and so on. For quick reference, turn to the Index of Letters by Industry and Job Title and the Index of Letters That Address Specific Issues at the end of the book.

In using the model letters provided, it's important that you personalize them so that they don't sound too generic. Remember to pay attention to visual appearance, as well. All of the text provided here can be used in letter or e-mail form, but you'll need to do some simple reformatting, cutting, and pasting in order to be certain that its appearance is appropriate for the medium you choose.

In addition to all the cover letters in the book, the downloadable content also includes Worksheets 3-1, 3-2, and 3-3 from Chapter 3 for those who prefer to complete these worksheets on the computer. What's more, you'll find expert tips, templates, and samples to help you create your own killer resume!

Downloadable Templates and Samples for Creating Killer Resumes

If you don't already have a resume to use in your job search, you can use the templates and samples included here to create your own. If you have one that uses a skills-based, achievement-based, or combination resume format, you should still prepare a resume in the chronological format. Not only is it generally required by most recruiters, human resource personnel and employers, but it also makes it easier to upload (by cutting and pasting) your job history and information to online job applications. The templates included here are general enough to work in a variety of settings; use them to guide you as you create a strong, focused, easy-to-read resume—one that will prove essential to networking, responding to job postings and ads, presenting in personal meetings and at interviews.

Included in the downloadable content, you will find:

- A template for a one-page Chronological Resume
- A sample resume using the one-page format
- A template for a two-page Chronological Resume
- A sample resume using the two-page format

Insider Tips to Guide You as You Create Your Own Killer Resume!

Like the killer cover letter, an effective resume gets read, gets remembered, and gets results. To do so, it should *include* the best of your talents, strengths, and accomplishments…*exclude* anything that distracts from these…and *present* you in the most positive, professional way. Here you'll find expert guidance and real-world examples to help you accomplish these objectives by focusing on the three elements integral to a killer resume: Profile, Content, and Format.

Links to Online Career Advice, Job Boards, Social Media, Blogging, and Professional Networking Sites

The downloadable content that accompanies this book connects you directly to descriptions of and hyperlinks to well-known and widely used online job search resources, including:

- Career and Job Search Advice Websites
- Professional Networking Sites
- Online Job Boards: General and Composite
- Online Job Boards: Niche and Industry-Specific

Access Instructions

Visit www.mhprofessional.com/mediacenter/ and follow the on-screen instructions to access downloadable content.

Jobhunting in Today's New World

OUR WORLD IS driven by technology and its ability to connect us. Virtually everything we do involves the Internet, especially our interactions with others. We talk, text, tweet, e-mail, message, conference, send videos, and video chat via phones, smartphones, tablets, laptops, and even built-in car phone systems. Rapidly evolving, ever-improving technology touches every aspect of our lives—and the revolution is still in its infancy. Naturally, the job search is no exception.

For jobhunters, the place to be is online. You can use the Internet to search for openings, build networks, create a personal brand and digital footprint, upload resumes, complete applications, and even interview. Most start-ups, entrepreneurs, and multinational corporations maintain active career centers on their websites, as do academic, political, government, and nonprofit organizations. Recruiters source, contact, and track candidates using systems and software that streamline the process, refine searches, and increase placement percentages. And of course, given the economic implosion that began in 2008, a vast number of search-related websites are generating substantial revenue from all this electronic activity, and new sites continue to be launched.

While so much has changed, some constants remain. Chief among them is the direct and indisputable link between the jobhunter's effort and the success of his or her search. Those who devote more time and energy to the process are the ones who are securing interviews and landing jobs, often more quickly. However, what is equally important is that, despite all the resources and capabilities that the Internet affords, sitting at the computer all day, every day rarely results in a job offer. Successful jobhunters wisely capitalize on virtual online communities to forge promising connections, then initiate actual conversations, attend actual networking events, and schedule actual face-to-face meetings. The fact is, networking is still the number one vehicle that drives jobhunting success—and you are in the driver's seat.

Today, you can count on technology to introduce access and opportunity to a process that most people find daunting, disheartening, and difficult. You can thank recruiters and hiring managers for maintaining a focus on the human side, the person at the core of the "search." What's up to you, then, is to tap the resources that are available to you, create optimal connections to people to whom you present the unique combination of strengths, talents, experience, and achievements that you, and you alone, have to offer. This book will help you accomplish just that.

The amount of information and the number of resources that are available to you online are quite simply staggering. It's genuinely impossible to calculate how many websites cater to those who are in the market for a job. This is partly because there are too many to count. And it's also because underutilized or underfunded sites shut down, successful ones are acquired by larger competitors, and new ones are launched every day. The bottom line is this: there is no excuse for not tapping this valuable source of information. So if you're not already familiar with using the Internet, search engines, social media, and e-mail, get serious about it. Take courses. Ask friends or family members, especially children and grandchildren. Read books (yes, there are books that can help, such as the "for Dummies" series that includes *The Internet for Dummies, Job-Hunting and Career Change All-in-One for Dummies, Job Searching with Social Media for Dummies, Job Search Online for Dummies, Job Interviews for Dummies*, and more).

Career and Job Search Advice

If you're not sure what type of job you want, or if you are considering a career change, start exploring online. Search possible job titles or industry names to get a general understanding of them. Search specific companies, organizations, and professional associations to discover how certain jobs fit into the organization's operations and bottom line. Visit job boards (described later in this chapter) to discover what a specific job entails, what you would be responsible for in that position, and what qualifications you'll need to have in order to be eligible for consideration.

You can also search online for professional career coaches who can assist you in determining an appealing and appropriate career path to pursue. Thanks to the Internet, you are not limited to those in your city, town, or region; geographic borders disappear online.

How to Find Job Openings Online: Job Boards and More

To uncover jobs in your area, specialty, or industry or at specific organizations that interest you, visit online job boards like Monster.com, Career-Builder, and TheLadders. These are just three of the hundreds of sites from which to choose; some of them list all jobs, while others target specific niches such as administrative staff, nursing, financial services, or nonprofits.

For example, *general* job boards include jobs of all types in all locations, industries, and sectors. *Composite* or *aggregate* job boards feature a sampling of job postings collected from other sites. *Niche* sites focus on jobs in particular industries, sectors, locations, affiliations, or other specific categories. Some of these are listed here; you'll find direct links to these and many others in the downloadable content that accompanies your purchase of this book.

With so many choices, it's easy to search by job title or by industry, state, region, city, or even salary level—and because most job boards include salaries, they are indispensable in determining realistic salaries or salary ranges for the positions you are seeking.

A Sampling of Career and Job Search Advice Websites

Career Rocketeer
Job-hunt.org
Careercast.com
Jobsearch.about.com
CAREERREALISM.com
Glassdoor.com
Careeronestop.org
Career-advice.monster.com
JibberJabber.com

For hyperlinks, please visit www .mhprofessional.com/mediacenter.

A Sampling of Online Job Boards: General

Monster.com
Beyond.com
CareerBuilder
TheLadders
EmploymentGuide
CollegeRecruiter
Craigslist.org
Jobs2careers
ClassifiedAds

For hyperlinks, please visit www .mhprofessional.com/mediacenter.

Job boards are not the only source of job listings online. Many companies devote space on their corporate websites to presenting career opportunities and job postings. The same is true for nonprofit organizations. You may also check the career centers on the sites of the high school, college, university, and graduate schools you attended and those of professional associations of which you are a member.

How to Connect to People Who Can Help: Professional Networking Sites

Professional networking sites like LinkedIn are proving increasingly productive. Not only are more jobhunters forging connections that are leading them to openings, referrals, and contacts, but many people now expect to be tapped for help, making it more comfortable for you to ask. So by all means, use these sites to build your own professional network.

Spend some time creating a strong professional profile, which, as a bonus, allows recruiters to find *you* when they search online for candidates with skills like yours, even if you were not actively looking at the position they are seeking to fill. Then forge connections with anyone who can:

- Provide information on a career or job that you are considering.
- Connect you to someone who works in an industry or at a company that interests you.
- Recommend you to fill a specific job opening.

Once you've developed a solid network, you might post an item of interest every few weeks, such as a recent accomplishment, a recommendation, or a link to an article or blog that presents a new or fresh insight on some aspect of your industry—always positive and upbeat rather than a complaint about the job market. The Internet makes it easy and fun to create this network. It also makes it easy for you to *feel* productive when you're sitting at your computer without necessarily *being* productive; keep in mind that it's not about counting how many connections you have. Ultimately, your objective is to propel your search from the faceless world of online jobhunting to the

> **A Sampling of Professional Networking Sites**
>
> ---
>
> LinkedIn
> Networking for Professionals
> Academia
>
> For hyperlinks, please visit www
> .mhprofessional.com/mediacenter.

real world, where you meet real people face to face and secure advice, additional connections, leads, interviews, and offers. That is what will make you, and your search, productive.

How (and Whether) to Use Social Media and Blogging Sites

Social media can be useful—but only if you are disciplined in your approach to them. As with professional networking, your goal is to make connections that will lead to an interview. If you are active on social media and blogging sites, and if you are connected to people who can help you on a professional level, these resources may help advance your search. If this is the case, you'll want to make sure that your posts and updates are never too personal, potentially embarrassing, or unprofessional. However, if your connections and posts are predominantly casual and unrelated to business, you are better off using professional networking sites for your search. (See more on maintaining your online presence in the next section.)

> **A Sampling of Social Media and Blogging Sites**
>
> Facebook
> Twitter
> Tumblr
>
> For hyperlinks, please visit www
> .mhprofessional.com/mediacenter.

How to Create and Maintain Your Online Presence

Using the Internet for your job search requires you to create and maintain an online presence. Creating it is easy: visit the social media and networking sites on which you wish to be accessible to others, such as LinkedIn, Facebook, and Twitter. These sites will guide you through the simple (though sometimes maddening) process of adding, writing, and uploading information, which typically includes your name, education, work experience, optional photo, recommendations, and preferences. Once you've created a profile, you can search for people you know who you can connect with in order to establish a networking base. Include appropriate friends, family members, current professional colleagues, and those you've worked with in the past. These connections will link you to others, and before long, you will have built a network that you can tap to identify potential employers, uncover openings before and after they are listed, and actively promote yourself in the search. (See Chapter 4 for specific guidance on networking.)

Maintaining your online presence, however, is entirely different. Enter your own name in a search engine like Google. You'll be surprised—and possibly shocked—by all that appears. You'll find links to the profiles you've created on social and professional networking sites along with comments you've posted on sites such as YouTube, Instagram, Tumblr, and Pinterest. You'll find links to photographs in which you were tagged online or named in a caption in print, such as newspaper articles, alumni magazines, or even church bulletins. If you've written blogs, articles, or books or appeared on television, you'll find links to these. Expect to see your name listed on the sites of boards, clubs, and associations of which you are a member. Your contact information appears on sites like WhitePages, with more links that for a fee reveal your background, police records, and other such information. You may see the stores at which you've created online accounts, references to yourself in newspaper articles that appeared decades ago, and possibly even the obituary of someone with the same name as yours! Combined, all this information serves as your "digital footprint," and it's of paramount importance in your search. It's what recruiters, your networking connections, and your next employer can—and probably will—use to form an impression of you based on where, how, and how often you appear online.

If what you find is not what you want others to see, the first step is to clean it up. Tailor, prune, and delete anything that creates a less than professional image. Remove, unpin, and untag yourself from any photos that may compromise your integrity. Delete posts containing questionable language.

E-mail addresses are part of your profile, too. You may have many, but the one you choose for your job search activity must sound professional. If you're using "iguanasaremylife@xxx.com," it's time to open an account with one of the major providers using your name. MaryBrown@zmail .com not only is more professional, but also helps hiring managers find you more easily when they conduct their own searches. When you have a strong professional profile, recruiters searching for someone with your skill set can find *you*!

Technology and the Internet have changed how and how often you conduct a job search, but not what makes that search effective. Your personal process remains the same: prepare yourself with a strong, achievement-oriented resume, killer jobhunting letters, a networking plan, and the determination to stay on track until you reach your goal. Let the search begin!

Guidelines to Speed Your Search

In addition to capitalizing on the opportunities afforded to you by technology and the Internet, here are additional guidelines to help speed your search.

Develop a 12-Month Plan

In today's challenging job market, many jobhunters are finding that the search is taking significantly longer than it did in the past. Regardless of what expectations you may have or may hear, assume a time frame of at least 12 months for your search. Then, set consistent and realistic daily objectives—ones that you can sustain throughout that period. Chances are, you'll find that your job search is less like a sprint and more like a marathon. Don't expect to reach the finish line in a day. Instead, expect to reach for and achieve daily goals, such as networking with 5 contacts per day or 10 new contacts per week. Without this attitude, you'll view every day as a laborious burden that does not produce results. You'll risk losing focus, motivation, and direction. You'll neither write nor interview well, and your search may take even longer.

Accept Help

Should your previous employer offer you the benefit of outplacement services, seize this valuable opportunity. Explore the resources of federal and local labor departments, the public library, and any associations, unions, or industry groups of which you are a member. Many organizations offer free training programs for which you may be eligible. Investigate every resource that's offered to you, and then decide which ones may suit your needs.

Assess Your Skills

Identifying your unique skills, strengths, and traits can be difficult. This is true not because you don't possess any, but because we so often take our own capabilities for granted. So spend some time considering your skills—or ask a friend or colleague to help you. Jot them down, from the most simple ("I can use both a PC and a Mac") to the more complex ("I am an expert in Microsoft Office, social media, and website design") to the truly astonishing ("I brought in $25 million in new business as a direct result of developing a Facebook page to attract and engage consumers"). Be sure to use the worksheets in Chapter 3 to help you—you can complete them electronically by using this link: http://www.mhprofessional.com/mediacenter. Once you've listed your skills, you can then decide which ones are relevant to the various positions for which you may apply. This becomes especially important if you're transferring skills to a new job or industry. In every case, identifying what you can do and what sets you apart from other candidates is essential.

Network, Network, Network

You can't start soon enough or do too much networking. You're planning your future, after all, so take charge! Begin by listing all the people to whom you can talk. Don't limit this to those who may have the job you want. *Anyone* and *everyone* can spread the word that you are—or will be—searching for a new position. Whether it's passing along your resume, providing a referral, connecting you to others on LinkedIn, or simply keeping you in mind should an opportunity arise to mention your name, there's something for everyone to do. As soon as you know you'll be looking, draft your list. Begin with the names of friends and family members. To that, add current work contacts, previous employers, coworkers, fellow alumni, and so on. Use your smartphone or tablet to record names, phone numbers, and

RECRUITER'S TIP > **How to Ride the Age Wave**

Whether you're 25 or 75, age may play a role in your job search, despite the fact that the law prohibits age discrimination. If you're working with a recruiter on a particular position, seek advice on how to handle age issues. Your youth may account for your desirable technological proficiency, your understanding of social media and industry innovations, or the ability to connect with prospects in your age group. Your maturity may suggest more in-depth knowledge or mastery, a historical perspective on your industry or specialty, or experience in managing people and change. Plus, energy, enthusiasm, and adaptability are ageless. So don't short-change yourself—get comfortable with your strengths!

e-mail addresses of those who are willing to offer assistance—you never know whom you'll meet, so be prepared. Develop an "elevator speech," and practice it out loud with someone you trust. It should explain—in a minute or less—your unique talents and experience, what you are seeking and why, and what benefits you can deliver to your next employer. Print up "business cards" to distribute at opportune moments; these should provide your name, e-mail address, address, phone number(s), and public profile address on LinkedIn and/or similarly appropriate professional networking sites, along with a very brief description of the type of position you are seeking. Seize every opportunity to network—including holidays, conventions, weddings, and reunions, when you're likely to encounter people you don't see regularly.

Follow Up Rigorously

In any jobhunting environment—but especially in a tough one—following up after an interview is imperative. It's a safe bet that most people don't write after an interview, and that if they do, they dash off predictable, trite e-mails or letters that do nothing to remind the interviewer of how singularly qualified they are for the positions they desire. So you must never fail to write a strong, well-planned follow-up message. You must also follow through with thank you notes to anyone who offered help and referrals or who served as a reference. In a tough market, the number of interviews you have may be limited. That means you'll have more time between them, and that deprives you of any excuse for not writing! Once your search is over (and it will be), be certain to inform *and thank* all those who offered encouragement, contacts, or support, and even those who were willing to help but didn't, for whatever reason. You never know when your next job search may begin.

Expect to Be Checked

Be sure to read Chapter 2, "The Top 10 Rules for Writing Killer Cover Letters." Every rule is vital to an effective job search. Recent events illustrate just how vital. Take the following rule, for example: "tell the truth or pay the consequences." This rule is crucial in light of today's corporate scandals, a by-product of which is the fact that background checks are now conducted with greater regularity and greater scrutiny—and the Internet makes it exceedingly easy to confirm everything in your background, as well as to accept jokes or rumors that may appear about you on social media sites as fact. Therefore, if there is anything questionable in your past or anything that might be misconstrued, don't hope that it won't be discovered. State it yourself—it's the only way you can control how this information is presented! Telling your next employer up front what she will discover anyway can only make you appear honest and trustworthy. If you're lucky, you'll find that your next boss is someone who believes that everyone deserves a second chance.

RECRUITER'S TIP ❯ **Money Makes the World Go 'Round . . . and Your Head Spin**

Conventional wisdom says that the person who mentions the first figure will ultimately lose in salary negotiation. So what do you do when an ad warns that "serious candidates will provide current salary and requirements"? Do some digging. Use the Internet to research salaries for similar positions in your area. Include the monetary value of benefits and bonuses in your calculation of current or past salaries to increase them. Or provide a salary range to avoid overpricing yourself. The Issue Index lists letters in this book with sample language that you can use.

Take Advantage of Technology

As we have just explained at length, the Internet offers unlimited and valuable resources for jobhunters. So be sure to take advantage of them. Peruse the sites that can help you define the type of job for which your skills are a match. Explore those that list jobs in your industry or your locale, those of specific companies, and those that provide salary ranges, which can prove helpful if you are relocating or switching industries. If you're not certain where to start, visit any search engine and enter the word *jobs* or *career* to find links that will connect you to thousands of valuable resources, or begin with the links that we provided in the downloadable content in this book. When you see jobs posted for which you are qualified, post your resume and cover letter in response. For sites that limit space, be prepared with a shorter version of your cover letter and resume. If a job posting reveals the name of the hiring organization, visit its website and apply directly on its career tab. While you are there, you may gain insight into the corporate culture that you can use in your interviews. Even better, you may find a direct contact and his or her e-mail address. Use it! If it's posted, it's available for you. Also look for websites hosted by associations within your industry or specialty, or your alma mater; such sites frequently maintain a job bank and a referral network or offer training. The Internet is an amazing source of information, career advice and assistance, company websites, job postings, and sometimes total confusion. If you haven't already, master this vital tool and use it to your benefit.

Manage Your Online Profile

Like all business, today's job search process takes place online. Most, if not all, openings are posted and filled online. Recruiters source, contact, and keep track of candidates using online searches and tracking systems. Used correctly, the online search offers numerous advantages. Of paramount importance is your online presence, your "profile." Your next employer can easily form an impression of you based on where, how, and how often you appear online. Research yourself just as he will; search your name, nickname, photos, and social media sites. If warranted, clean up what your find. Pay particular attention to the pictures you post and the language you use to be certain that they convey the image you want. When you have a strong professional profile, recruiters searching for someone with your skill set can find *you!*

Learn How to Use E-mail Effectively

Obviously, if you don't already know how to use e-mail, do whatever you need to do to learn. Not only has it become ubiquitous in the workplace, but e-mail delivers advantages that can prove pivotal for your job search. For starters, making cold calls or attempting to secure face-to-face meetings with busy executives is increasingly difficult, if not impossible, given ever-tightening corporate security. With e-mail, networking has become far, far easier. Use e-mail to stay in touch, check in periodically, send articles or relevant news items, and even gently prod someone to take action on your behalf. Every few weeks, you can e-mail those in your network base to remind them that you're still looking and what your areas of interest are. Should you change or narrow your focus, you can quickly update your career "fan club" about this important information.

When surfing the Internet's many job search websites, you'll find plenty of advice on using e-mail effectively in the job search. Here are a few key points and potential pitfalls relating to jobhunting letters of which you'll want to be aware.

Option 1: Letters as Attachments You may send your cover letter as an attachment, rather than, or in addition to, inserting it into the body of the e-mail. Saving it as a .pdf, Word, or Google document increases the likelihood that your recipient will receive your letter exactly as you've created it. All the letters and e-mails in this book can be downloaded, customized, saved in your own word processing program, attached, and sent successfully. If you plan to include your letter in the body of your e-mail, you should avoid using line breaks, multiple fonts, and other formatting that may alter your letter's appearance if it is opened in a different program or window size. These are precisely the types of changes that can result in a letter that makes you appear sloppy and unprofessional.

Option 2: Letters Within E-mail Messages The fact that e-mail is the preferred method of communicating presents both a challenge and an opportunity.

A primary challenge is that readers are busy and may not take the time to read a long letter. Another is that they may not even open it! For these reasons, your subject line is key—it must be strong, appealing, descriptive, appropriate, or all of these, and you'll want to write a short, concise note. Although short is the standard in e-mail, short doesn't mean dry, boring, jargon-filled, or devoid of content. You still need to follow all the advice you'll find in Chapter 5 about promoting your skills, accomplishments, strengths, and personality. To create effective and professional e-mail cover letters, familiarize yourself with this list of formatting tips and the sample e-mail letter that follows. (See Letter 1-1.)

- Use the subject line to refer to the position you are seeking.
- Use a consistent font size (10 to 12 points).
- Do not use bold, italic, underlining, columns, long dashes, or other unusual characters.
- Use an asterisk (*) or a plus sign (+) instead of bullets.
- Use the spacebar to indent, rather than the tab key.
- Avoid hard-to-read and trendy fonts; instead, select the more common Cambria, Calibri, Times New Roman, or Arial.
- Add the recipient to your electronic address book in such a way that his or her name appears—not his or her e-mail address.

LETTER 1-1   E-mail Resume Cover Letter—Webmaster

From: Barrett Peters
To: Carol Rodriguez

Sent: Monday, October 7, 20XX
Attachment: Barrett Peters Webmaster Resume
Subject: Your Opening for a Webmaster

Descriptive subject line

Greetings. I hope you will take a moment to read the resume I've attached to this note, as I'm certain that you'll find in it the skills and strengths you are seeking in a Webmaster.

Friendly, professional opening avoids "To Whom It May Concern"

As you'll see, I have developed and maintained sizable websites for several Fortune 500 organizations, including HealthForum USA, Costal Petroleum, and DiversCo. What's more, your firm will benefit from my unusual combination of experience and personal strengths:

Common font

+ Recognized as a disciplined, yet caring leader who can manage teams both large and small that work remotely or onsite.
+ Exceptional proficiency with multiple platforms and technologies.
+ Highly effective at communicating with colleagues, clients, and C-suite executives.
+ Successful at working in a high-pressure, fast-paced environment.

Formatting simulates indentations

I've attached my resume for your review and will contact you shortly to see if we might meet in person. In the meantime, please feel free to contact me at any of the numbers I've listed below.

Takes initiative to contact recipient and . . .

Sincerely,
Barrett Peters
bpeters@bpm.com
(123) 456-6789 home
(098) 765-4321 work
(111) 222-3333 cell

. . . provides complete contact information.

If you can secure your reader's physical address, you have the opportunity to increase the chances that your cover letter will get read, get remembered, and get results by sending it via "snail mail" instead of, or in addition to, the e-mail version. This way, your reader can view your letter with the proper, professional formatting that you prefer. Since most people never think of taking such a step, you instantly set yourself apart from your competition. In addition to supplying an actual (not virtual) version of your qualifications, this also affords you a second opportunity to present your reader with your skills, strengths, and the benefits you can deliver!

Here is the formatting to use when sending letters via "snail mail."

LETTER 1-2   Snail-Mail Resume Cover Letter—Webmaster

Monday, October 7, 20XX

Ms. Carol Rodriguez
Chief Technology Officer
MileHigh Communications   RE: Your Opening for a Webmaster
1234 Main Street
Denver, CO 09876

Dear Ms. Rodriguez:

To follow up on an e-mail I sent earlier this week, I have enclosed my resume with this letter to be certain that it does not get overlooked. I hope you will take a moment to read it, as I'm certain that you'll recognize the skills and strengths you are seeking in a Webmaster.

As you'll see, I have developed and maintained sizable websites for several Fortune 500 organizations, including HealthForum USA, Costal Petroleum, and DiversCo. What's more, your firm will benefit from my unusual combination of experience and personal strengths:

- Recognized as a disciplined, yet caring leader who can manage teams both large and small that work remotely or onsite.
- Exceptional proficiency with multiple platforms and technologies.

- Highly effective at communicating with colleagues, clients, and C-suite executives.
- Successful at working in a high-pressure, fast-paced environment.

I will take the liberty of contacting you shortly to see if we might meet in person. In the meantime, please feel free to contact me at any of the numbers I've listed below or via e-mail.

Sincerely,

Barrett Peters

Barrett Peters
bpeters@bpm.com
(123) 456-6789 home
(098) 765-4321 work
(111) 222-3333 cell

Enclosure: Barrett Peters Webmaster Resume

The Top 10 Rules for Writing Killer Cover Letters

As TEMPTING AS it may be, sending only your resume in response to a job ad or posting is not as effective as sending a cover letter or e-mail as well. The good news for you is that many people succumb to this temptation—some of them out of laziness, and some because they don't trust their writing abilities. The bottom line is: these days, a resume isn't enough.

In today's job market, a resume doubles as a sign that indicates, "I need a job... like so many others... thousands of others." In this environment, your resume alone cannot possibly accomplish as much as you need to accomplish. Although it reveals vital statistics, your resume supplies only 20 percent of the information on which most hiring decisions are based. It reveals whether you meet the minimum requirements for the current opening (appropriate education, computer skills, or relevant experience, for example). It also suggests to your next boss the level of loyalty and continuity that can be expected of you, as demonstrated by the length of time you've held previous positions. Finally—and especially in a tough economy, resulting in an overflowing inbox—your prospective employer may attempt to reduce the list of candidates to a manageable level. In this case, your resume may actually work *against* you by providing a single fact or date that serves to eliminate you as a potential employee.

Furthermore, regardless of how exceptional your resume may be, it generally reveals none of the remaining 80 percent of the information upon which the hiring decision is based. It says nothing about your personality, creativity, or work style. It rarely describes any unusual traits you possess that might make you a sterling candidate or interesting interview material. A letter, on the other hand, can reveal all of this—and more.

> Throughout this book, the word *letter* refers to any and all types of written communication, including e-mail, handwritten notes, and even typed letters sent via "snail mail."

For all of these reasons, the letters you send as part of your job search may be some of the most important letters you'll ever write. To help you create a winning letter, let's begin with the basics. Let's take a look at a typical employment advertisement and the typical response it generates.

Sample Employment Ad or Job Posting

> ### ATTENTION SELF-STARTERS!
>
> This is your opportunity to build success from the ground up. Enjoy the full training and technical support that only a major financial services firm such as ours can offer as you help businesses and individuals plan sound financial futures. Write Terry Muldour at tmuldour@recruiter.com.

In today's economy, an ad like the one shown here may receive more than 1,000 responses! From this pool, as few as fifteen candidates may make it through the first screening to a personal meeting. Of these, a mere six people will probably be called for a second interview. Two or three will be selected as finalists. One will be hired.

Who will that person be? Certainly *not* the one who sends in a resume with Letter 2-1.

LETTER 2-1	Resume Cover Letter Sent in Response to Advertisement (Poor)

Ms. Muldour:

In response to your job posting online, I have attached my resume for your consideration. It is my objective to obtain a position in the economic area of your company. I recently received my MBA after completing a BS in Economics with a Business minor. I have an extensive background and strong working experience.

I would be very interested in working for your company due to the fact that it would permit me to utilize my business and economic background. In my six years of study, I have developed my knowledge of econometric analysis, price analysis, financial management, strategic marketing, branding, and business management. I am currently developing a paper on the treatment of global trade tariffs that uses a dynamic process and a flexible functional form to determine the variables affecting treatment differences between developing and developed countries. Working in a financial firm for several years enabled me to become a more committed leader, a team player, a detail-oriented worker, and better communicator who is not afraid to devise and implement effective strategic management theories. My responsibilities included researching the backgrounds of individuals and companies wishing to open sizeable credit accounts overseas. In addition, I have much additional working experience, including being a management trainer and busboy at a major dining establishment in New York City. I am a hard worker and a team player, as you will see when you interview me. My resume highlights my educational and business background.

Attached is a copy of my resume for your consideration. Please don't hesitate to contact me at any time for an interview. I am certain that you'll find it of great interest to meet me due to my natural leadership qualities, vision, and solid experience in your area of business.

Sincerely,

Philip Tucker

Because the majority of the people responding to this ad will not send a cover letter at all, simply sending this gives Mr. Tucker an advantage over the competition. The advantage is all but wasted, however, by sending a letter that's as weak and unappealing as this one.

As you read Letter 2-2, the stronger version of the same letter, you'll see the differences—and the improvements they make in the effectiveness of the letter.

LETTER 2-2   Resume Cover Letter Sent in Response
to Advertisement (Better)

Greetings, Terry Muldour:

You're looking for a self-starter to work in the financial field—I'm a self-starter with financial <u>expertise</u> and <u>experience</u>!

My resume, which is attached, details my background; let me provide you with the highlights:

<u>Thorough educational background</u>: I recently received my MBA after completing a BS in Economics with a Business minor.

<u>Firm grasp of finance</u>: In my six years of study, I developed expertise in econometric and price analysis as well as marketing, branding, and financial and business management.

<u>A proven self-starter:</u> I am currently writing a postgraduate paper on global trade tariffs, for which I created my own unique research methods and models.

<u>Financial work experience</u>: By investigating individuals and companies wishing to open sizable credit accounts overseas, I became a dedicated leader, a detail-oriented worker, and a highly effective communicator.

I am a hard worker and a team player. I have the knowledge, skill, and desire to enhance the success of today's financial company. If you will contact me at (555) 456-7890 during the day or evening, I will make myself available at your convenience for an interview.

Thank you for your consideration. I look forward to meeting you.

Sincerely,
Philip Tucker

PTucker@zmail.com
(555) 456-7890

If you've hired someone yourself, you may recognize the weaknesses of the first, poorly presented letter—and the strengths of the second, stronger one. If you haven't hired anyone, approach the letter as you might a solicitation for a charitable contribution, a type of letter that attempts to be equally convincing. Which of the two letters would you be more likely to read through to the end? Which makes a better impression? Which candidate would you be more likely to interview?

10 Basic Dos and Don'ts for Writing Killer Cover Letters

The two preceding letters provide concrete, visual examples of the 10 basic dos and don'ts to follow in all your jobhunting correspondence.

1. Dress (Your Letters) for Success
Do Send Professional Letters; Don't Send Form Letters

Do make every e-mail and letter you send clean and professional looking. Even the smallest typo is an insult to the reader. It implies that he or she is not worth the time it would take to spell-check or to correct the error. It suggests that you are a sloppy person who doesn't value order, either personally or in the workplace. Recruiters spend a good deal of time advising jobhunters on how to dress for an interview because employers demand clean, orderly staff members with professional demeanors. Your letter should reflect these characteristics.

Do not allow any letter to appear to be a form letter. Your reader should not feel as though you are sending the same letter to hundreds of employers—even if you are! Instead, create the impression that you are sending a letter to a specific person for a specific reason: because you believe that there is an ideal match between you and your prospective employer. Standard lines such as "I want to work for your company" are meaningless to an employer, particularly if you haven't mentioned the name of the company—and they are worse when included in a letter to a recruiter—a mistake made by the writer such as in Letter 2-1. If you really want to work for a specific firm, you must have a reason. State it.

2. Zoom, Don't Resume
Do Make Your Letter Different from Your Resume

If your resume is strong, it will provide the information your interviewer will need. (If it's not, there are plenty of books, software programs, and professional resume writers out there to help you strengthen it—including the downloadable Resume Kit that comes with this book!) So don't just regurgitate your resume in letter form. "Zoom in" on the most salient points of your resume. Even better, consolidate the facts in your resume into an overview statement. Summarize a benefit that you offer such as "solid employment record," "extensive industry experience," or "impressive record of achievement." Guide your reader in forming an appropriate impression of you even before you meet. Letter 2-2 illustrates this principle. Best of all, turn this summary statement into one that suggests an advantage that your next employer may gain by hiring *you* instead of someone else.

Describe any special qualities you have that may set you apart from other candidates. Use language that creates a feeling of what kind of person you are. If you have a sense of humor, don't be afraid to show it in a professional way. You'll find examples in the sample letters throughout this book.

3. "In Response to Your Ad" . . . Not!
Don't Use Standard Openings

Many people think that only one type of letter is acceptable in the business world: one that follows a standard outline. In truth, the only type of letter that's acceptable in the business world is an effective one. An effective letter accomplishes your objective, which in the case of jobhunting letters means standing out from your competition. With this goal in mind, why send a letter that's likely to mirror the letters of those against whom you're competing?

Letter 2-1 opens with a standard line: "In response to your job posting online, I have attached my resume for your consideration." What's wrong with this opening? It's standard. To stand out from the competition, your letter should be anything but standard. In Letter 2-2, Mr. Tucker grabs the reader's attention immediately with a different, stronger opening. Furthermore, he successfully weaves information from the job posting into the opening to suggest that the letter was written in response to a specific ad and is not a form letter.

Do not open your letter with a standard, predictable statement. Spend a few minutes analyzing what is important to the person to whom you're writing. Peruse the sample openings provided throughout this book. There's no need to be foolish, outlandish, or shocking. With thought and practice, you can create unique, informative letter openings that will grab attention and deliver a meaningful message.

4. "Kiss" Your Letters (Keep It Simply Stated)
Do Write a Person, Not a Letter

There are also many people who believe that making a letter sound businesslike means using stuffy, stilted language that's full of clichés and jargon. Certainly, your letter should be professional. However, it must also be interesting, be appealing, and reflect your personality.

To create a letter that's appropriate to the business world, include relevant facts and succinct language. Ensure correct spelling and proper presentation. To make your letter appealing, use the same tone of voice you would use during the interview—when you don't have time to consult a thesaurus and replace the words you'd normally use with multisyllabic synonyms. Write with the attitude that you're writing to a person. That person may be your interviewer, your next boss, a human resources executive, or a recruiter—*but it's a person.* Before you write, try to picture that person. Try saying out loud the points you wish to make as if you were sitting face to face in an interview, and then jot them down. Flesh out these ideas into full sentences that reflect the way you speak. After all, your interviewer will want to meet the person to whom she was introduced in your letter, and it had better be you!

For a clear example, look back to Letters 2-1 and 2-2 by Philip Tucker. Letter 2-1 is replete with foggy jargon, leaving you without a single clear opinion of the candidate—except that he is likely to be boring. Letter 2-2 has introduced you to a person who has studied and is currently writing a research paper, an individual with personality traits that sound appealing—someone you might not mind interviewing, which is, after all, the purpose of the letter.

You'll find words and phrases to avoid using in your letter writing listed in Chapter 10.

5. Elim-Me-Nate

Do Focus on the Needs of Your Prospective Employer

What do you talk about in your resume? Me. Me. Me. Me. What do you talk about in your interview? Me. Me. Me. Me.

So use your letter to address the needs of your next employer. Focus your thoughts on the needs of your next boss. After all, your prospective employer expects you to meet *his* needs on a daily basis. Why should he care what your employment objective is or what you're looking for in a job? He will hire you and pay you for the specific contribution you will make to increasing profits, improving performance, or enhancing productivity. In the letter, tell him how you'll accomplish this.

Successful jobhunters create letters that link their strengths and talents to the benefits they will bring to the firm, department, team, or supervisor with whom they'll be working. Chapter 3 is devoted entirely to illustrating how to achieve this crucial goal.

6. Appealing Is Revealing

Do Make Your Letter Easy to Read

The visual appearance of a letter is as vital as its content, maybe even more so—because if you're lucky, your reader will devote 30 seconds to your letter before turning to the next one in the pile or inbox. Make it easy to skim. Note that Letter 2-1 is boring in appearance. Its italic print and fully justified margins make it difficult to read. On the other hand, Letter 2-2 is visually appealing. Its content actually appears to be interesting, and the letter can be scanned by the eye in seconds. The reader who spends 30 seconds on Letter 2-2 will form an instant, positive impression of the candidate.

How do you make a letter appeal to its recipient before he or she even reads it? Formatting. To illustrate its power, compare Letters 2-3 and 2-4.

LETTER 2-3   Resume Cover Letter (Poor Format)

Dear Chief Financial Officer:

To maintain continued growth, a company must have financial and management professionals who are capable of identifying and seizing market opportunities before the competition does.

My marketing savvy and management expertise can help you do just that. I possess a powerful commitment to task, a drive for excellence, and the ability to respond to customer needs. For example, in my current position, I increased sales 74% by upgrading service efficiency, resulting in a 25% annual increase in profitability. I streamlined a branch outlet from its inception, coordinating every aspect from recruitment to organizing and redefining office functions, thus achieving substantial cost reductions, greater efficiency, and increased market share. I reduced receivables from 115 days to 33 days, thereby improving cash flow 21%. This released enough working capital to enable the firm to expand into other markets. Because I am currently seeking to broaden my horizons, I eagerly await your reply so that we can arrange a personal meeting. Then we can discuss in greater detail how my particular blend of capabilities, experience, and managerial strengths can help your firm capture lucrative business opportunities.

Sincerely,

But take this letter word for word, format it differently, and the results are astounding.

LETTER 2-4 **Resume Cover Letter (Strong Format)**

Dear Chief Financial Officer:

To maintain continued growth, a company must have financial and management professionals who are capable of identifying and seizing market opportunities before the competition does.

My marketing savvy and management expertise can help you do just that. I possess a powerful commitment to task, a drive for excellence, and the ability to respond to customer needs. For example, in my current position:

- I increased sales 74% by upgrading service efficiency, resulting in a 25% annual increase in profitability.

- I streamlined a branch outlet from its inception, coordinating every aspect from recruitment to organizing and redefining office functions, thus achieving substantial cost reductions, greater efficiency, and increased market share.

- I reduced receivables from 115 days to 33 days, thereby improving cash flow 21%. This released enough working capital to enable the firm to expand into other markets.

Because I am currently seeking to broaden my horizons, I eagerly await your reply so that we can arrange a personal meeting. Then we can discuss in greater detail how my particular blend of capabilities, experience, and managerial strengths can help your firm capture lucrative business opportunities.

Sincerely,

The difference between Letters 2-3 and 2-4 is not in the wording. The content of both letters is identical. The difference is in the formatting. Letter 2-4 employs many of the same techniques that marketing and branding experts use to get millions of consumers to notice, absorb, and act on promotional messages. You can use the same tricks in your letters, which are equally promotional. Here are just a few of the more powerful options available to you.

- Don't use long paragraphs; they are overwhelming to the eye. (This will help you write more succinctly, too.)
- Indent sections with key ideas by using bullets, dashes, or asterisks to set them off (like these indented tips).
- For important ideas, use **bold**, <u>underlining</u>, and UPPERCASE LETTERS.
  - For short sentences, try centering.
- Use numerals (20) rather than spelling out numbers (twenty) when describing your accomplishments, to attract more attention. (Exception: Always spell out numbers that begin a sentence.)
- *Italics are hard to read; use them sparingly, if at all.*
- In printed letters, adjust your margins so that the reader never has to read more than five inches from left to right across a page. Never justify your right margin. (Always justify left margins.) If your letter must run to two pages in length, end the first page in the middle of a sentence to encourage the reader to read on to the second page.

If these techniques seem too pushy to you, remember that marketers have been using them for decades *because they work!*

7. Until It's a No, It's a Go!
Do Write Frequently

Your competition hates to write as much as you do. Chances are that most of the people who are vying for your next job will find numerous excuses to avoid writing jobhunting letters. Don't make the same mistake. You should write these letters often. Always send a thank you letter for a referral, and a follow-up letter after a meeting or an interview. If your candidacy seems to have stalled, write again to make something happen—don't allow yourself to be forgotten. You might send your prospective employer an additional reference or a recent newspaper article supporting an issue that you discussed during your interview. As far as you should be concerned, until you get a definite rejection, you're still in the running. In many cases, this perseverance and follow-through are essential requirements for the job you want.

8. Tell the Truth or Pay the Consequences

Don't Be Dishonest

Do not exaggerate, mislead, or lie in your letters. Even if you get hired, dishonesty is grounds for immediate dismissal. Don't risk it.

9. Check, Recheck, and Triple-Check

Do Triple-Check Your Letters for Proper Presentation

If you're new to the jobhunting process, you will find the following reminders helpful.

Do direct your letter to the reader. Remember Terry Muldour from the sample employment ad earlier in this chapter? It was impossible to discern from the ad whether Terry Muldour was male or female. In fact, some recruiters purposely make an ad vague to test the resourcefulness of the jobhunter, a ploy that Terry Muldour may have used. If you are faced with this ambiguity, don't rely on the standard "To Whom It May Concern" salutation, because it's standard. Try to contact the company in question or visit its website to obtain the information you need. If that fails, use the entire name (as did the writer of Letter 2-2) or the person's title (as did the writer of Letter 2-4).

Do check your spelling before you hit Send. Poor spelling creates a sloppy, negative impression quickly. Always spell-check. Ask a friend to proofread your letter. Proofreading backward from the end to the beginning will help you catch errors that you might overlook when reading forward.

Do be sure to use the same heading (or "masthead") on your resume and on the letters you attach to e-mails or upload to websites—one that includes your name, address, e-mail address, and the telephone number(s) at which you can be reached. You may also include the online addresses of your profiles on professional networking sites.

Do check to be sure you've included keywords in your letters as well as your resume and your application when responding to online job postings.

The job search is not the time for accidental mishaps that can jeopardize your success. Chapter 10 contains a checklist to help you avoid such mishaps and to ensure that your letter is strong, direct, and properly presented.

10. If It Ain't Working . . . Fix It!
Don't Keep Using a Letter That's Not Working

You've composed a resume cover letter, sent it in response to 10 postings and ads, and haven't heard a thing. Not a single person has called; not one interview has been scheduled. Is it you? Is it your resume? It could be either. Or it could be that you're perfectly qualified, but your cover letter isn't making the impact you want. Worse, it might be hurting you.

Don't despair. Writing about yourself is never easy, and (until you've read this book) you've never been taught how to write self-promotional letters. Jobhunting letters may be some of the most difficult letters you'll ever create.

So if the letter you're using isn't working, try another approach. You can try a more unusual subject line or first line, or try adopting a bolder tone of voice or a more conservative one. You can also summarize your strengths more succinctly, or provide a bit more detail. The key is to try something *different*. Rewrite portions of your letter, and then send this new letter to a limited number of people to gauge its effectiveness. If you don't get the results you want, try changing something else. It may take a while, but don't allow yourself to get discouraged.

By doing such things, you're employing the same tested marketing techniques that advertisers have used for ages. How many approaches and slogans has McDonald's used? Or Ford? Or Verizon? These companies and their advertising agencies continually alter their strategic positioning to keep their profits up, their objectives met, and their goals achieved. Why shouldn't you do the same?

How to Identify and Sell Your Strengths

WHATEVER INDUSTRY YOU represent, whatever field you're in, or whatever expertise you possess, when you're looking for a job, you're in sales and marketing.

- You're selling a product: you.
- You identify the target market: potential employers.
- You price the product: a realistic salary range.
- You position the product: draft a resume and cover letter.
- You test your positioning with the target market: respond to several job postings. If your efforts result in interviews, you've probably done some decent marketing. If not, you'll need to reassess your product, market, pricing, or positioning and try again.

This is precisely the process that marketing executives follow to sell laundry detergent, pickup trucks, gourmet cat food, club memberships, and retractable swimming pool covers.

Thus, the majority of the letters you'll write in the course of finding your next job will contain self-promotion. In your Ad Response and Resume Cover Letters, you will trumpet your talents. After an interview, a Follow-Up Letter will once again reaffirm your excellent qualifications. If the hiring process seems to be idling, you'll rev that engine with a reminder of your unique talents. And undoubtedly, if you attempt to negotiate your salary in writing, your special skills will be of vital importance.

Since self-promotion is an area in which recruiters have found most people to be either underwhelming or overwhelming, it pays to learn how to boast. It *is* possible to be modest, yet effective. The trick is to avoid speaking solely of your own merits in every line. Instead, link your talents to the concerns of the recruiter, employer, or firm. Think of your qualifications not as merely a feature of your candidacy, but as a *benefit* to your next boss. The worksheets that follow will help you accomplish this.

Take the time to complete Worksheets 3-1 and 3-2 right now. The ideas you jot down here will prove extremely useful later on, when you are creating your own letters—whether you follow the guidelines offered in the chapters to come, or whether you simply adapt the sample letters that are included throughout the book. Completing these worksheets will also help you crystallize your thoughts in preparation for an interview.

RECRUITER'S TIP > **God Preferred ... Others May Apply**

Don't be afraid to answer ads and respond to job postings if you have most, but not all, of the qualifications required. Recruiters often describe the "ideal" candidate in employment ads to see whether anyone can attain this perfection.

Your skills—and your experience in applying them—may be the best combination that companies and recruiters can find. Let them decide.

Worksheet 3-1: I Am ... Because I ...

In the left-hand column of the worksheet, list your skills, strengths, unusual abilities, unique traits, areas of expertise or specialization, and relevant personality traits. Try to limit your entries to one or two words each.

In the right-hand column, jot down your support points. Rather than repeating the facts on your resume, expand on them while relating something new, different, or additional. Consolidate your facts by adding

---

Go directly to Worksheet 3-1, or complete this and the following two worksheets electronically by using this link: http://www.mhprofessional.com/mediacenter. You'll find instructions for using the link to download valuable resources at the back of this book.

together years in the field, jobs within an industry, or similar positions
you've held at different firms. Summarize your career, education, experience, or personality. Follow the examples set by the three sample entries.

Worksheet 3-1

I Am
(Your skill, unusual ability, unique trait,
or area of expertise)

Because I
(How you acquired this particular strength)

I am *a skilled worker*   because *I worked at your leading competitor for over 15 years.*

I am *well versed in process improvement methodologies*   because *I participated in Lean Six Sigma training.*

I am *experienced in heavy equipment sales*   because *I was the number two biller at John Deere for 3 years and a top biller at General Motors for 10.*

I am _____ because I _____

I am _____ because I _____

I am _____ because I _____

I am _____ because I _____

Worksheet 3-2: So You...

With that done, you're now ready to seize a powerful advantage over your competition.

In their letters, those whom you're competing against are certain to include the type of facts you've written in Worksheet 3-1—facts like "I am a skilled worker" and "I am well versed in process improvement methodologies." Although these statements may be true, if they are standing alone, they require recruiters and employers to do all the work, that is, to interpret what they will mean to the company and discern why they are beneficial.

Go directly to Worksheet 3-2, or complete this and the other two worksheets contained in this chapter electronically by using this link: http://www.mhprofessional.com/mediacenter. You'll find instructions for using the link to download valuable resources at the back of this book.

You, however, can easily handle this for your reader. Simply ask yourself, "What does this mean to my potential employer?" Instead of just stating that you are a skilled worker, translate this fact into a benefit, such as, "so you won't have to train me." To the statement "I am well versed in process improvement methodologies," you might add, "so you save training time and money because I can begin being productive for you from day one." If you have chosen to cite the fact that you rarely take sick days, translate this into "Because I rarely take sick days, you can count on adding a highly reliable worker to your support staff."

Go directly to Worksheet 3-3, or complete this and the other two worksheets contained in this chapter electronically by using this link: http://www.mhprofessional.com/mediacenter. You'll find instructions for using the link to download valuable resources at the back of this book.

Therefore, to complete Worksheet 3-2, think about the benefits you can offer your next employer based on the statements that you made in Worksheet 3-1. For each "I am" and "because I" that you included in the preceding worksheet, add a corresponding, "And what this means for you is" in Worksheet 3-2. As a guide, relate these benefits to the areas that are of greatest concern to employers: profits, productivity, and performance.

Once you've completed Worksheets 3-1 and 3-2, you've identified your strengths and the facts that support them. More important, you've linked them directly to benefits that you can offer your next employer. Now you have successfully created unique ideas that you can introduce

---

Worksheet 3-2

. . . And What This Means for You Is
(What benefits your skills, special traits, or background offer your next employer; what positive difference or improvements you can make)

. . . so you *will save time and money, since you won't have to train me.*

_____

_____

. . . so you *will have a worker who can begin reducing expenses and boosting profits from day one.*

_____

. . . so you *get a sales representative who can hit the ground running.*

_____

_____

. . . so you _____

_____

_____

. . . so you _____

_____

_____

. . . so you _____

_____

_____

. . . so you _____

_____

_____

in your jobhunting letters. The sample letters in this book will provide many examples of how to do this.

Or, try to combine your entries from Worksheets 3-1 and 3-2 into full sentences. You can either use the sentences word for word or reconstruct

---

Worksheet 3-3

How to Use This in Your Letter:
Benefit Statement Options

I am _____ because I _____.

What this means for you is _____.

Because I _____ , I am _____.

What this means for you is _____.

Because I _____ , I am _____,

so you _____.

You (so you) _____ because I _____

_____ , and I am _____.

You (so you) _____ thanks to my

(I am) _____ , which I developed/became/achieved through/as

(because I) _____.

Through (because I) _____ ,

I have developed/built/become (I am) _____ ,

and that means you _____.

Throughout my (because I) _____ ,

I achieved/succeeded in/produced/excelled at (I am) _____.

As a result, you/The result is that you (so you) _____.

them into alternative forms. The options on Worksheet 3-3 demonstrate how many ways there are to build a sentence describing the benefits that you offer an employer.

Sample Benefit Statements

The following sentences have been composed from the three sample entries in Worksheets 3-1 and 3-2. Each sample uses one of the constructions outlined in Worksheet 3-3. For easy reference, these samples use the options in the same order in which they appear in Worksheet 3-3.

- I am a skilled worker because I worked at your leading competitor for more than 15 years. What this means for you is that you will save time and money, since you won't have to train me.
- Because I worked at your leading competitor for more than 15 years, I am a skilled worker. What this means for you is that you will save time and money, since you won't have to train me.
- Because I worked at your leading competitor for more than 15 years, I am a skilled worker, so you can save time and money, since you won't have to train me.
- You will have a worker who *can begin reducing expenses and boosting profits* from day one because I participated in Lean Six Sigma training and I am well versed in process improvement methodologies.
- You get a worker who *can begin reducing expenses and boosting profits* from day one, thanks to my knowledge of process improvement methodologies, which I developed through my participation in Lean Six Sigma training.
- Because I was the number two biller at John Deere for 3 years and a top biller at General Motors for 10 years, I have become experienced in heavy equipment sales, and that means that you get a sales representative who can hit the ground running.
- Because I am experienced in heavy equipment sales, I achieved superior results at John Deere and General Motors. As a result, you get a sales representative who can hit the ground running.

Sample Benefit Statements Adapted for Different Industries

The preceding samples illustrate how three different people might build a variety of sentences from their completed Worksheets 3-1 and 3-2. Now take a look at how these same sentence construction options might be adapted for use in other industries. Although your field may not be one of those represented here, perusing these examples will demonstrate how you can adapt them to your own field.

Engineer: I am a skilled electronics engineer because I worked in General Electric's Consumer Division for four years. What this means for you is that you will save time and money, since you won't have to train me.

Arts: Because I worked at the Smithsonian Institute for more than 12 years, I am a highly experienced curator. What this means for you is that you will not need to be understaffed for weeks while training a novice to assume full curatorial responsibilities.

Sales: Because I worked at your leading competitor for more than 15 years, I am experienced in all aspects of selling telecommunications to growing businesses, so you can expect more immediate revenue growth from your sales team.

Sales: You get a sales representative who can hit the ground running, thanks to my experience in retail promotion, which I developed as a top account executive for Procter & Gamble.

Beautician: You will have a worker who is productive from day one because I studied at the Avalon Beauty Academy, and I am knowledgeable in all aspects of hair styling and coloring.

Sports: Because I was the senior ski instructor at Aspen Ski Resort for seven years, I have become proficient in dealing with the public, and that means that you get a representative who can significantly enhance customer relations.

Technician: Because I am well versed in maintaining vertical transportation equipment, I achieved superior ratings at Otis Elevator.

As a result, you acquire a technician who can minimize unproductive downtime for your high-profile corporate clients.

Use Worksheets 3-1, 3-2, and 3-3 and the preceding examples to create your own self-promotional sentences. Write one for each quality you will be promoting in your job search. Then, link these sentences together.

Voila! You have just written a paragraph (or two) that will constitute the body of many jobhunting letters.

Sample Letters/E-mails

By completing the worksheets, you have taken an essential step toward writing killer cover letters. As you incorporate the paragraphs you have just written into your letters, you are fulfilling the second rule from Chapter 2's "10 Basic Dos and Don'ts for Writing Killer Cover Letters": "Zoom, Don't Resume." This rule requires that you focus on your potential employer's needs rather than simply repeating the information listed in your resume. This advice holds true regardless of your industry, and the following sample letters illustrate this key point.

Take a few minutes to read these sample letters. You'll discover that they are very similar to one another. Each has been written in response to a job posting or employment advertisement in a different industry. Each is from an applicant in a different situation. They are presented here to illustrate that such details become immaterial when a letter "sells" a candidate, and how that candidate's skills might benefit a potential employer. Cover letters like these grab *and keep* a reader's attention. They stand a far better chance of resulting in an interview than the traditional, standard cover letters that most people send.

Most of the sample letters included throughout this book illustrate this key principle. As you review them, you may be surprised at how little industry-specific or job-specific information is included. Therefore, be sure you don't overlook letters that seem to be outside your field—virtually every letter in this book contains an idea you can use.

LETTER 3-1 ▶ Resume Cover Letter—
Customer Service Representative

It's twice as hard to attract a new customer as it is to maintain an existing one. Unfortunately, this fact is often overlooked by many businesses.

Delivering high-quality, responsive service is vital in banking, and that's exactly what you'll get when you hire me.

As my resume indicates, I have worked in financial services for more than three years, so you won't have to go to great expense to train me. Plus, I have learned how to deal with a wide variety of people, from the pleasant senior citizen to the irate executive. In every case, I assess their needs and how the bank can address them most effectively. The vast majority of my customers have walked away content. More important, they have <u>returned to do business with us again</u>.

If you're looking for an experienced professional to provide superior service and promote customer satisfaction, you've found her. I hope you'll give me a call at (555) 456-7890 so that we can meet. Thank you for this opportunity to discuss my qualifications.

Sincerely,

LETTER 3-2   Resume Cover Letter—Cable Repair

When a customer calls for a repair, your firm is faced with an opportunity. Either the client relationship will be cemented, or it will be damaged. The difference, as you know, is in the hands of the repair technician.

The ability to deliver high-quality, pleasant service is vital in telecommunications, and that's exactly what you'll get when you hire me.

As my resume indicates, I have worked as a technician for more than three years, so you won't have to go to great expense to train me.

Plus, I have learned how to deal with a wide variety of people, from the pleasant senior citizen to the irate executive. In every case, I assess the complaint, the equipment problem, and how I can address both most effectively. The vast majority of the customers I have served have been pleased with my responsiveness and my professional demeanor. More important, they have continued to do business with my employer.

If you're looking for an experienced professional to provide superior service and promote customer satisfaction, you've found him. I hope you'll give me a call at (555) 456-7890 so that we can meet. Thank you for this opportunity to discuss my qualifications.

Sincerely,

LETTER 3-3   Resume Cover Letter—
Travel Agent—Workforce Return

I am responding to your ad because it offers the opportunity to act on a very firm conviction of mine: that every business is a service business and, to succeed, must address the distinct needs of each and every customer.

The ability to deliver high-quality, responsive service is vital in the travel industry, and that's exactly what you'll get when you hire me.

My resume, which is attached, details my background. Although I have been out of the workforce for several years, I have hardly been idle. As a hospital volunteer, president of the PTA, wife and partner of a senior vice president, and mother, I have dealt with a wide variety of people, from the pleasant senior citizen to the screaming child to the irate executive. In every case, I assess the individual's needs and how to address those needs most effectively.

As a very active consumer, I am well aware of the importance of prompt, attentive service—and painfully aware that it is rare these days. If you're looking for a hard worker and a quick learner to provide superior service and promote customer satisfaction, you've found her.

I hope you'll give me a call at (555) 456-7890 so that we can meet. Thank you for this opportunity to discuss my qualifications.

Sincerely,

LETTER 3-4 ▶ Resume Cover Letter—X-ray Technician

Delivering high-quality, responsive service is vital in healthcare, and that's exactly what you'll get when you hire me. As my resume indicates, I am licensed in this state and board-certified. I have worked in clinics and in private practice for more than seven years, so you won't have to train me.

Plus, I have learned how to deal with a wide variety of patients, from the pleasant senior citizen to the nervous mother and the terrified single woman. In every case, I have provided comfort and reassurance along with clear instructions and a gentle touch.

In fact, the vast majority of the patients who I have worked with have walked away pleased with their care. More important, they have returned for their annuals year after year.

If you're looking for an experienced professional to provide superior and proper care while dealing effectively with a diverse patient base, you've found him. I hope you'll give me a call at (555) 456-7890 so that we can meet. Thank you for this opportunity to discuss my qualifications.

Sincerely,

CHAPTER 4

The Networking Letter

IN ANY ECONOMIC ENVIRONMENT—especially a challenging one—networking is indispensable. It is the most effective way to uncover opportunities, secure interviews, and land jobs. Thankfully, online professional networking communities make it easier than ever for you to identify and connect with those who can help with your search. Once you do connect, following up with a strong and persuasive networking letter is critically important.

How to Use E-mail to Identify (or Create!) Job Opportunities

To appreciate the edge that the Networking Letter affords you, consider the marketing principle of action versus reaction. Translated to the search process, this principle characterizes people who *react* as those who wait for job openings to be announced and advertised, then apply and wait again to be called in for an interview. Most jobhunters fall into this group, and they are your competition.

Conversely, those who *act* create their own opportunities. They hunt down potential and existing job openings and go after them with vigor, often identifying such openings well before they are advertised. Becoming someone who *acts* rather than *reacts* places you in an important minority: that of confident, proactive networkers. This is exactly where you want to be to enjoy a vital advantage in today's tough job market. As a proactive networker, you have priceless tools at your disposal in the networking letter. Use these tools wisely and frequently. Use them

---

RECRUITER'S TIP ⟩ **A Whole New World**

The Internet has changed everything for jobhunters. Enter "job search" in your browser, and in less than a second, you'll be presented with more than three billion links! Instantly, you can find openings, advice, guidance, professional resources, support communities and forums, recruiters, resume services, and much more. Take advantage of all the benefits this new world has to offer. No matter what age you are, what industry you are in, or what your level of experience or education may be, your search will take place online. Don't be overwhelmed—it's become easier than ever.

Fact: Only 25 percent of the people who landed full-time jobs learned of the openings through employment ads. The remaining 75 percent secured employment through active networking.

Networking is work... but it's work that works.

---

to introduce yourself and to ask for advice, contacts, or a referral to an associate or colleague. Use them to identify openings before they are advertised, such as when colleagues switch jobs, companies move to a new location, or businesses expand. Even a company that is downsizing may hold promise if it is consolidating positions. Two specialized workers, for instance, may be replaced with one who can handle multiple responsibilities. You can use these letters to uncover this strategic information and more.

If a friend suggests that you write to an acquaintance for assistance, accept. If a blog or a newspaper or magazine article reports that a company is expanding into new markets or relocating to your area, write and

---

RECRUITER'S TIP ⟩ **Go! Get Set! Get Ready!**

Getting ready to get ready can be very costly in the jobhunting process. Start networking as soon as you know that you want to make a move or suspect that you may need to.

Make a list of people you can contact immediately, and then do so. Search online for more connections. If your resume is out of date, a scheduled interview is all the motivation you'll need to get your resume in order.

No resume, no research, no excuses!

RECRUITER'S TIP 〉 **Why Do I Contact Thee? Let Me Count the Ways**

Use your networking letters to:

1. Introduce yourself.
2. Seek advice.
3. Make contacts.
4. Secure a referral through an associate or colleague.
5. Identify openings before they are advertised.
6. Follow up on hiring leads gleaned from blogs or from newspaper or magazine articles.
7. Learn more about a field you'd like to enter.

And much more!

---

ask to be considered. Ask friends and family members about openings where they work—many organizations offer financial bonuses for referring candidates who are hired. What's more, sites such as Employee-Buddy.com and Jobs2Web.com connect jobhunters with employees at companies that offer such compensation—truly a win-win for all! Don't avoid creating and capitalizing on such opportunities because you don't want to write a networking letter. Use the letters and e-mails provided here as a guide to presenting yourself as a qualified, motivated candidate who searches for ways to make things happen. In almost every case, these qualities are highly sought after in the job market.

Whatever your reason for writing it, your networking letter is fundamentally an appeal for help. Your *primary* goal—in fact, your *only* goal—is to get your reader to comply with a reasonable request for assistance. You might ask for an introduction, a recommendation, advice, or ideas. To comply, your readers must give of their time, share knowledge, and put their names or reputations on the line by making referrals—all precious commodities. To achieve your goal, you've got to convince your readers that you're worth this effort.

Use the steps that follow to guide you in creating effective networking letters. If you choose to use sections of the letters provided in this book, you can use these steps to adapt the samples for your own use.

Step 1: Create a Connection

To enhance the speed and effectiveness of your networking, you should send the networking letter to numerous people simultaneously. The trick, of course, is to make each letter sound as though it is being sent *only* to the person receiving it—your letters should never look or sound like form letters.

In your effort to personalize each letter, capitalize on any connection you may have with the reader. You may share an area of expertise. You may belong to a common professional association, online community, or civic, sports, religious, or charitable organization. You may have originated from the same area of the country or have attended the same educational institution. Now is the time to reaffirm these connections. Mention a mutual friend or a recent telephone conversation you had with your reader. If you met at a party or business event, remind her of the encounter.

Use this information to open your letter. Identifying a meaningful link between yourself and your reader helps establish a personal connection. Because this suggests to the reader that only he can help you, he will feel more compelled to focus on and reply to your request.

Step 2: Inform

To accomplish your primary goal, which is to elicit help, you must convince your reader that what you are offering is meaningful. If you're asking for a referral, you must be worth referring. If you're asking whether there might be an opening for someone with your skills, those skills must be relevant to the firm, the division, or the person to whom you're writing. Keep in mind that recommending an unqualified candidate reflects poorly on the person referring you. Don't put anyone in this awkward position.

Therefore, in the body of your letter, provide the information your reader needs to have in order to make the decision to act on your behalf. Describe your talents, your background, and your skills. Explain why they are meaningful to your prospective employer, whether it's the person you're writing to or the person to whom you'd like to be introduced. And remember not to repeat what's on your resume word for word, particularly if you'll be attaching or enclosing it.

How much space should you devote to this information? Supply as much data as it takes to make your point convincingly, and no more. If the person to whom you're writing is not the one who will be making the hiring decision, keep your letters short and to the point. To secure a referral, for example, your reader needs to be assured in a general sense that you will not turn out to be unqualified and, therefore, an embarrassment to her. Paint an overview of yourself that demonstrates that you have the necessary experience to be a serious candidate. When describing your background, generalize. When discussing your accomplishments, summarize.

However, if you're introducing yourself to someone who does have the direct authority to hire you, you may wish to offer more detail. In this case, be specific about what you can bring to the corporation, the team, or your supervisor. Where relevant, use facts and figures to make your case—ones that you can honestly support in an interview. Instead of listing your skills in a vacuum, link them to concrete benefits that they offer your next employer. You may wish to refer back to the worksheets in Chapter 3 for pointers on how to do this.

In the samples that follow, you'll see examples of networking letters that are both brief and lengthy. As you read them, try to discern the reason each writer may have had for contacting each recipient. Apply this to your own circumstances, and you'll create a more effective letter.

Step 3: Request Action

You've established a personal connection. You've convinced the reader that you rate the time and energy required to comply with your request. Now, forge a bargain with the reader: "I'll do the work, if you're ready with what I need."

If you haven't already asked for whatever it is that you want, now is the time to do so. State straight out exactly what you need, and how the reader can help you. Don't annoy your reader by beating around the bush. You should be polite, but also direct. Your reader should not have to spend time deciphering puzzling innuendoes. If you're writing to introduce yourself, say so. If you're writing to ask for a referral, say so. Above all, don't ask for something that's inappropriate.

Then, *tell the reader what to do*, and be specific. If you've asked him to contact you, provide him with your address, e-mail address, and telephone number, along with a time that is best to reach you. If you require confidentiality, say so. Make it as easy as possible for your reader to reach you. If you're asking that something be sent to you, include your e-mail address.

Or, if *you* are the one who will take action, *tell the reader what to expect.* State exactly what you will do to facilitate a response. If you plan to contact your reader, say when, how, and why. If you're visiting from out of town and would like to meet with your reader, state when you'll be in town and when you'll be available. If possible, offer several alternative dates and times.

Optional Step 4: Close Warmly

It's highly advisable to end your networking letters with a professional, yet friendly sign-off. Closing warmly—by thanking the reader in advance for complying with your request—frequently enhances the likelihood of your getting the response you seek. You'll find examples of such closings in the sample letters that follow.

Sample Letters/E-mails

LETTER 4-1   Networking—General—Layoffs

May I ask a favor of an old fraternity brother?

The writer establishes the connection...

You see, in one way or another, this volatile economy affects us all— and now it's my turn. Yes, I'm one of the 240 loyal employees that my firm has just laid off. So now I'm exploring options throughout our industry, including the possibility of launching a business of my own.

informs...

tells the reader what to expect...

Your advice and perspective, Bill, would be very helpful to me as I decide what my next step will be. I'd appreciate it if you could spare some time to share your thoughts with me.

On the 25th of this month, I'll be in your area and would love to buy you lunch. I'll call next week to see if this is convenient.

and closes warmly.

Thanks in advance—hope to see you.

LETTER 4-2 ▸ Networking—Economist

As a 10-year member of the Economic Forecasting Association, I am writing with the hope that our organization might assist me in my job search.

I am an experienced agricultural economist, with a specialty in soy and soy by-products, seeking employment in either the private or the public sector. I realize, of course, that I am not alone in my quest. However, as a prolific author, I can offer my employer a very high level of positive visibility within the industry.

I would appreciate any advice you can offer. Does EFA, for example, maintain a job bank? Do you run a referral service? Perhaps you or an associate know of someone with whom I might speak for additional advice.

I would welcome any suggestions you can offer. I have attached my resume and a list of my published works for your information. To make matters even easier for you, I will plan to call you next week.

Make it easy for the reader to comply.

For your interest and assistance, I am deeply grateful.

Your fellow member,

This enterprising rising star has used e-mail to get directly to someone who is in a position to help or hire her. Her thoughtful and engaging letter is strengthened by the artful single-line teaser in the middle of the letter.

LETTER 4-3   Networking—Branding

Subject: Thank You for Your Encouragement

Congratulations on the favorable publicity you received in yesterday's *City Times*. I'm sure I'm not alone in finding encouragement in the description of your journey to senior management in the technology industry, an industry of which I am proud to be a part—although I haven't achieved the success you have.

Yet.

As a hard-working, highly skilled, and dedicated Associate Account Executive for a boutique branding firm, I am anxious to expand my capabilities by assuming greater responsibility. I would greatly appreciate it if you could spare a few minutes of your time to discuss with me the direction that our dynamic industry will take over the next few years and what someone with my interests could contribute.

I've attached my resume to demonstrate my commitment to hard work. I will take the liberty of contacting your office within the next few days to see if there might be a convenient time for us to meet. Thank you in advance for being willing to assist someone who would be proud to follow in your footsteps!

LETTER 4-4   Networking—Sales—Career Change

A mutual acquaintance, Shirley Louis, recommended that I contact you for advice. I am currently exploring the possibility of switching from computer to medical equipment sales. With your expertise and recent experience entering this field, you have insight that could prove extremely valuable to me.

I've attached my resume, which details my skills and background, along with a list of my accomplishments. I expect that several of my strengths will be quite transferable, such as attention to detail and the ability to work with complex technology. I would welcome your views on this observation, as well.

Knowing how busy you are, I would be most grateful if you could spare a few moments of your day for me. I will call your office shortly to arrange a meeting at a time that is convenient for you.

With appreciation,

Although the writer is not required to provide this information, she feels that the reference to daycare will alleviate any concerns her reader may have about her reliability.

LETTER 4-5   Networking—Healthcare—Workforce Return

I am writing at the suggestion of Francis Myers, a maternity nurse on your staff and a close friend of mine. Francis thought that your needs and my talents would fit ideally, and that we should meet.

By way of introduction, let me explain that I am returning to nursing after a three-year absence. During this time, I had a son and relocated to the Boston area. Now that I have made arrangements for daycare, I am seeking to put my skills back to work where they are needed: in a burn unit. My **solid training** and **in-depth experience** have both focused on the care of burn victims, and I would like to return to my nursing specialty as soon as possible.

I will take the liberty of calling you next week to see if we might meet. If you would be kind enough to leave word with your assistant, I will schedule a meeting at your convenience. In the meantime, I thank you in advance for your consideration.

Sincerely,

LETTER 4-6   Networking—Financial

What a small world! Ten years ago, you and I both worked at Morgan Stanley, and now our paths have crossed again. It was great seeing you at the broker-dealer luncheon last week; I appreciate your offer to pass my name along to your ETF team.

To this end, I've attached my resume. As you'll see, it details the considerable experience I've enjoyed on the sell side, including my key role in the launch of funds transfer systems for two major investment banks.

As you no doubt recognize, this kind of hands-on expertise can prove immensely valuable for your firm. It means that I am equipped not only to forecast the challenges that lie ahead as our industry continues to evolve, but also to create the <u>innovative solutions</u> demanded of those institutions that will succeed in the years to come.

I am making plans to visit your area from the 5th through the 10th of next month and would be grateful for some of your time. I will call your office shortly to set up a meeting.

Thanks again, Bill, for your support.

LETTER 4-7   Networking—Arts—Student—Career Change

Because you graciously added your name to State University's Alumni Career Network, I am writing with the hope that you might spare a few minutes to advise a fellow alumnus.

I earned my BS in Accounting at State, and I have since enjoyed a successful career in the sales and marketing of consumer electronics and telecommunications. Now, I would like to bring the strengths that this solid background offers to a new field. Your role in the arts community could provide a perspective on this transition that would be of great value to me.

Because I would appreciate the opportunity to gain the benefit of your insight, I will take the liberty of calling you next week to see if we might meet or simply speak on the phone. In the meantime, I have attached my resume to provide details.

I am grateful for your willingness to help fellow State graduates. I thank you in advance for helping me, in particular.

Most sincerely,

This is actually a combination networking and "make something happen" letter; notice the writer's clever suggestion to overcome the interviewer's hiring objection.

LETTER 4-8   Networking—Arts—Career Change—Job Loss

Meeting you was a real pleasure. Thank you for spending so much time with me, particularly on a Friday evening. I truly appreciate the advice you gave me and the contacts you offered.

Since our meeting, I have reworked my resume according to your recommendations; a copy is attached. I am thrilled with the new emphasis and have forwarded it to Maestro Richard Allen at City Orchestra, as you suggested. I will let you know the results of these efforts.

I am dismayed that you are not currently able to hire an assistant. Not only would it be a pleasure to work with you, but I am certain that my corporate background could open new doors for the Symphony. Should my experience produce the level of additional funding I anticipate, the position of assistant would certainly pay for itself!

Ever the optimist, I will keep in touch with you in the event that the Symphony's financial status improves.

Thank you again for your kind assistance.

With best regards,

LETTER 4-9   Networking—Financial—Job Loss

When last we met, we spent some time discussing the Dodd-Frank Act. Lo and behold, shortly thereafter, our legislators enacted the Volcker Rule, reinstating some of the provisions of Glass-Steagall!

Therefore, I thought you'd be interested in seeing the attached article, featured in the *Economist*'s current issue, which analyzes the new legislation's impact in the hedge fund space. Obviously, now is the time for devising proactive strategies to keep this profitable market from further eroding, and the article highlights the actions that several investment firms have already taken.

I thought of you immediately upon reading this article because I found our discussion so enlightening. I also appreciate the interest you expressed at that time in my attempts to further my career. I am continuing my search and will keep you informed. In the meantime, should your firm's hiring freeze be lifted, I hope you will think of me. Your organization has been at the top of my wish list for years, and after meeting you, I am certain that our association would be immensely productive for us both.

Thank you again for your interest.

All the best,

LETTER 4-10   Networking—Financial

It was a pleasure meeting you at last week's retirement seminar. The amount of work that went into preparing such an informative program was evident and well spent, I can assure you. Your presenters held the interest of each participant, and clearly described the products and services that your firm offers.

Given my background and my interest in this area of financial services, I believe that I may be able to offer your firm something of value in return. As the enclosed resume demonstrates, my track record with prospective customers is a proven one; over the last 16 months, I have increased our company's sales of retirement planning services by 22%!

This is the growth potential I would like to offer a leading firm such as yours. If you have any advice or recommendation to offer, I would be most grateful. I will take the liberty of calling you shortly to see to whom I should address my credentials at your organization.

Again, my thanks for a most enjoyable seminar and for any assistance you can provide.

With appreciation,

This letter may produce freelance work, a referral, or an interview. Any of these could lead ultimately to a job. That's effective networking.

LETTER 4-11 ▸ Networking—Public Relations—Social Media—
Job Loss

It was with great alarm that I read in today's *Wall Street Journal* that you are forced to curtail your promotional capabilities. Undoubtedly, today's economy wreaks havoc without regard for individuals, families, or profits. Despite this unfortunate situation, may I offer a glimmer of hope?

With reduced staff and financial resources, it becomes even more essential to generate **free publicity**, and to do so requires an expert.

I can deliver this critical service without an office at your headquarters, without an administrative assistant on your payroll, and without costly healthcare benefits. For a modest per-project fee, I am available to identify newsworthy developments, and to draft press releases, blog articles, and social media posts and place them with appropriate media representatives for **maximum, free exposure**.

Note the killer close!

Mr. Dupree, in today's challenging economy, the need for publicity is more vital than ever. Don't let your firm drop from sight—or worse, receive only the negative attention that results from a story such as today's *Journal* piece. I will call shortly to follow up.

Sincerely,

This writer obviously knows her reader well, so a familiar tone of voice is an appropriate choice.

LETTER 4-12 Networking—Website Design—Social Media— Career Change

---

It is hard to believe how long it has been since we have been able to sit down and talk. How about scheduling lunch (on me) before another day passes? Here's my ulterior motive right up front: I have a thought on which I'd like to get your advice.

Since we started working together over a decade ago, things have changed dramatically. Technology, people, places, and things seem to be in a constant state of flux. (I suppose this is what makes life interesting.) Through this flux, my firm has remained alive and well, continuing to break new ground in the world of website design, content, and user engagement. Nevertheless, I have been giving some thought to relinquishing the security of a staff position for the freedom of self-employment.

Perhaps, in your travels through the winding roads of corporate America, you may have heard what firms are outsourcing design work, if any. Are companies likely to rely on freelancers for design projects, or will they acquire staff members with an eye toward cutting costs? These are the questions I'll need to answer before making my decision. I know your viewpoint will be beneficial.

I'll call you early next week to set up a lunch date. Can't wait to see you.

A nice, soft approach.

Best,

LETTER 4-13 ▸ Networking—Telemarketing

You may recall that last May I had the pleasure of working with you when you were at AmeriBrands for several weeks. I was delighted to hear from our mutual friend, Mark Miller, that you might be looking to hire a telemarketing sales supervisor.

No one can dispute your firm's supremacy in its field. I believe, as I am sure you do, that superior telemarketing is an integral part of J. J. Budd's continued success. After four very successful years at Ameri-Brands, I am now looking for new challenges in the telemarketing industry. I would like a chance to be part of your telemarketing sales team—and to achieve for J. J. Budd the impressive results that I have attained for AmeriBrands.

As my resume indicates, during my four years as a sales manager with AmeriBrands, I consistently earned a place on the list of Top 10 Sales Managers. I also trained and ran the farm data TSR team that achieved the lowest cost per order among three competing vendors.

For a number of months, I have worked with Mark Miller. Mark can vouch for my abilities to motivate TSRs and achieve high sales at a low cost. Please feel free to talk with him. (Mark's number at work is 800-555-7654, extension 123.)

I will give you a call in the next day or two to see if there is a convenient time we can meet to discuss how my accomplishments might benefit you and your organization.

Very truly yours,

LETTER 4-14 ▸ Networking—General

Thank you for your warm response to my cold call! It is gratifying to know that there are, indeed, executives who remember their own early career struggles.

As promised, I've attached my resume and a list of my accomplishments. Any advice you can offer on the presentation of both would be most appreciated—as is your kind offer to introduce me to your colleagues.

Together, my education and experience equip me to grasp quickly the intricacies of the business world. My talents allow me to apply this knowledge to the ways in which I can most directly contribute to your profitability and performance.

I will follow up shortly to discuss your reaction to the enclosed materials. Thank you again for your consideration.

Sincerely,

This extremely enterprising student has set her sights on the firm she wishes to join after graduation and the executive she believes will usher her in the door. She's certainly not afraid of working hard to get what she wants, as this letter demonstrates.

LETTER 4-15   Networking—Student—Environmental Sciences

Redfield Industries' striking profit margins have captured the attention of everyone in the business world—and I am no exception. Congratulations!

Although the story behind this tremendous growth has been told over and over by the media, no one has focused on your contributions, Ms. Seifert.

As staff writer for State University's respected daily newspaper, I would like to focus on your perspective as a female executive, and the unique way in which you have contributed to Redfield's success. Rest assured, I will not waste your time. Not only have I done my research on the company's track record, but I am also an Environmental Sciences major with a special interest in the groundbreaking innovations that Redfield Industries has introduced in alternative energy, in which you played a key role.

I would be honored if you could spare some time from your busy schedule to speak with me. I will call you shortly to see when we might meet.

Thank you in advance for your time.

Sincerely,

LETTER 4-16 ⟩ Networking—General

When I heard through the grapevine that you had joined FronTech, I was thrilled for you! I know that you've been anxious to find the ideal position, and I truly hope that this is it.

Although FronTech has a sterling reputation, I know that you'll find some way to improve its standing. After what you achieved for MVRS, I can only say that the competition had better look out!

And, since I currently work for one of those very competitors, I thought this might be the perfect time for us to be on the same team. (After all, if I can't beat you, I might as well join you.) If you are or will be in a position to add to your staff, I hope you'll keep me in mind. As you know, my track record is exceptional, my achievements legendary, and my motivation as strong as ever. (OK, so my modesty needs work.)

Before you get ensconced in management meetings, let me buy you lunch. We'll celebrate your new job and explore what the future may bring. My treat.

I'll call you next week.

Best,

This quick note uses humor to let friends, family, colleagues, and others know that you need their help networking for a new job.

LETTER 4-17   Networking—General—Job Loss

Subject: Hello and help!

Hello. I hope this note finds you well and happy with your life, work, and play. I'm writing to let you know that today's tough economy has claimed another job... mine! I had the honor of being selected to join a talented pool of employees who will get the axe at the end of the month, and so I am currently in the market for a new position. From what I hear, though, companies are beginning to hire again—and I'm pleased to say that I have an entire resume's worth of skills and accomplishments that would make me an asset to many organizations. (And now that I've attached it to this note, you have it, too!)

Should you know anyone in the _____ industry, I would truly appreciate it if you could pass along my name and resume. Or let me know names and numbers, and I'll take over, using your name or not, as you prefer. As I keep my chin up (and my expenses down), I thank you in advance for any assistance you can offer.

Enjoy your day!!!

LETTER 4-18 Networking—Internship—Student

I am writing you at the suggestion of my father, Jon Omura, with whom you are a member of the Winchester Club. My father has spoken highly of your firm's internship program, and as a result, I would like to explore this unusual opportunity further.

For a Business major like me, such a program would offer valuable hands-on experience in the real world. More important, the chance to learn from experts such as those you employ is the chance of a lifetime.

Mr. Smith, would it be possible for you or one of your colleagues to spare some time to speak with me about your unique summer program? I have attached my resume to assure you of my strong qualifications.

I will take the liberty of contacting your assistant next Tuesday morning to see whether I might set up an appointment.

I thank you in advance and send my dad's greetings.

Sincerely,

LETTER 4-19 ▸ Networking—Training

What a thrill it was to participate in your productivity seminar last week. My congratulations on a highly informative and very entertaining presentation. I am quite certain that if my department placed as much emphasis on our clients' perceptions as you do on presentation materials, we would be far more productive!

This is exactly what leads me to write to you. Observing you in action reminded me of my past life in training. Through repeated promotions, I have been elevated away from my real loves: instructing, identifying, mentoring, and developing potential among bright, eager minds. I guess the more I crunch numbers, the more I lose sight of the people producing them, and it's been long enough.

Before I leap, I should make sure there's water in the pool, so to speak. Here's the deal: I buy you lunch; you endow me with your view of the training game. I would be really grateful to hear your views. I'll give you a call next week to see whether you can make the time for me.

And thanks again for a stirring presentation.

Best,

LETTER 4-20   Networking—Restaurant

It's been a while since we've seen one another. I hope all is well with you, Linda, and your two spunky boys!

You may have heard that I recently married and now have a baby on the way—and this is why I'm writing. Now that I am a family man myself, I am searching for a position in the restaurant/hospitality business that is more career-oriented, one that offers benefits and security.

As part of my search, I am writing to my colleagues and friends to see whether anyone might be aware of hiring activity, either current or planned. If so, I would be grateful if you could pass along my name— or let me know whom to contact.

After working in this business for seven years, you know my broad-based experience and the skills I offer. (My resume is attached.) I am an industrious worker who takes interest in my work and pride in my performance.

Any assistance you can provide will be greatly appreciated.

All the best,

The Ad Response and Resume Cover Letter

AD RESPONSE AND Resume Cover Letters serve a critically important purpose: they create the context in which your resume will be read.

Imagine, for example, your next boss reading through the many facts, figures, dates, and descriptions on your resume. In a busy work environment with regular interruptions, the risk is great that he will overlook or misinterpret information and hastily relegate your resume to the "do not interview" pile. Disaster.

Now imagine that, rather than leaving it up to him to pay attention, process the information correctly, and decide that you are worth interviewing, you lead him to this conclusion yourself right from the start. That's precisely what a well-written cover letter does! Its presentation of your qualifications, credentials, and accomplishments enables the reader to recognize the value that they offer him quickly and easily. Reading your resume after that, he interprets the details as proof of the conclusion you drew for him in your letter.

How to Create a Letter That Sets You Apart from Your Competition

For this reason, it is imperative that you spend time creating a killer cover letter. Use the samples in this chapter as is or as guidelines for writing your own letter or e-mail. To make your reader want to meet you and to interview you, help her make a connection between your talents and the

71

needs of her organization. The worksheets in Chapter 3 demonstrate how to link your specific skills with the needs of the hiring firm.

Since you use a more personal, conversational tone in your cover letters or e-mails than you do on your resume, they can bring you to life as a three-dimensional person who is interesting and unique. Referring to your background or current interests creates an impression not of a collection of facts and dates, but of a person who is worth meeting—*you*!

As you peruse the samples included here, you'll discover that virtually every one of them features an opening line that you may think of as somewhat unorthodox. Think again.

Step 1: Get Attention

Your ad response or resume cover letter arrives in your prospective employer's inbox in one of two ways: either it arrives unsolicited, such as when you send your resume after hearing about an opening or through a referral, or it arrives with hundreds of other resumes from your competition, such as when you answer an ad or a job posting.

Once it does arrive, it's fighting for attention against all those other resumes and letters, plus the usual reports, memos, solicitations, newsletters, and spam. The person to whom you are writing may give your note only 5 or 10 seconds for a quick scan before hitting "delete." As a result, you've got to win that reader's concentration immediately. There are no second chances.

Forget the standard openings you used to use—you know, the ones that are used by the vast majority of jobhunters, such as, "My name is Joe Smith, and I am applying for the sales position listed online," or, "In response to your ad in the *Daily Times*, I am submitting my resume for your consideration." While these openings may be appropriate for use with some highly formal firms and industries, or when writing to foreign organizations, they are wasted opportunities for most people who are jobhunting in a competitive economy.

Instead, begin your letter with a strong opening line that suggests to the reader, "Hey, read me!" Or, even better, "Don't hire anyone until we've met, and I'll tell you why."

The first line of your letter or e-mail should accomplish one of three objectives. The first is to *promise a benefit* to the reader. Tell your next employer what advantages you'll bring to him, such as any unique skills you possess, a rare perspective you offer, or a proven record of accomplishment. If your fluency in a second language is pertinent, mention it. If you are familiar with new platforms, systems, software, or equipment, include it. Just be certain that what you offer is meaningful to the firm and to the position you seek—and that you can really deliver what you promise.

A second way to open your letter is to *identify a need* that your reader has. For example, your reader may be searching for someone with mastery of a specific application, medical procedure, production process, or piece of equipment. Perhaps the need is for someone who is already familiar with the ins and outs of the business, the industry, the competition, or relevant government regulations. If you're writing to an accountant looking for an assistant, for example, you might open your letter with: "As a CPA, you know the importance of keeping abreast of changing government regulations. In my position with the New Jersey legislature, I managed such information on a daily basis."

A third objective for your opening is to *be timely*. Use your opening to relate news or new information. Refer to a recent event or issue of concern. Tie the end of the old year or the beginning of the new to the opportunity you offer for a fresh approach. Where appropriate, mention a new law, trend, report, or article or the current economic climate.

> **RECRUITER'S TIP > Re: The Re:**
>
> Recruiters often post more than one job opening at a time. Rather than sacrificing a strong opening line to refer to the ad you're answering and where it appeared, incorporate this information into your e-mail or letter. (See Letter 5-1.) Simply add "RE:" at the top of your letter or use the subject line of your e-mail like this:
>
> RE: Your Monster Posting for an
>   Office Manager

Killer Openings

The following sample openings illustrate each of these three objectives.

Promise a benefit.

- In the last 12 months, I've generated $70K in new business for my employer, and now I'd like to do the same for you.
- As a designer skilled in creating visually appealing, easily navigable, and engaging websites, I can provide the support your staff needs to bring in new business while saving you money on outside consultants.

- Integrity. Motivation. People Power. That's what it takes to be a successful manager. And that's what you get when you hire me.
- Your ad for a translator caught my attention immediately. *Pourquoi? Perche? Porque yo soy la persona perfecta para la posición.*
- They say there's no rest for the weary. So if you're weary from overwork, forget the rest of the candidates. Hire a proven professional, like me, who can relieve you of your overwhelming workload and help you get the rest you deserve.

Identify a need.

- For the opening in your production department, why not consider an expert who has spent the last three years mastering state-of-the-art film equipment at MTV?
- You're seeking a hard worker... I am one. You need retail experience... I've been in the business for 15 years! You ask for references... I've got plenty.
- If you're looking for a top-notch dental assistant, look no further.
- The match between your needs and my talents is ideal. Why? Because...

Be timely.

- No one has money to burn in a tough economy—which is why adding one exceptional research pro to your staff can actually reduce your overhead. Allow me to explain.
- If the federal government approves the revision of PL-1442 next month, you'll require the skills of a collections agent who has dealt with hazardous waste—a rare expertise that I'd be pleased to offer you.
- Congratulations on your recent promotion! With the additional responsibilities this entails, you may need an assistant with the special expertise I can offer you.
- In today's economy, there's no time to waste on workers who need continual training, motivation, and fires lit under them. Why not hire an experienced self-starter like me?

Step 2: Inform

Devote the main part of your letter or e-mail to supporting the promise you made in your opening. Explain why the person or company should consider, interview, and hire you. If you have completed the worksheets in Chapter 3, you already have several strong concepts to use. If you haven't completed these worksheets, take a few minutes to do so now, or follow the guidelines given here.

First, detail any specific skills, talents, or knowledge that you have and the difference that this will make to the firm—without repeating point by point what's on your resume. If your abilities might help your immediate superior reach his goals, say so. If you're switching fields, explain the benefits that this offers your prospective employer, such as a new perspective or the opportunity to expand into new areas.

Then, describe how you will deliver the benefits you've promised or how you acquired the special skills you possess. State what experience has taught you and how you learned. If you accomplished relevant goals in previous jobs, use this to support your claim; where appropriate, use dollar amounts and percentages of growth or increase. (And be sure you can substantiate them if you're asked to do so during the interview.) Relate your work experience to the skills you acquired, not to your job responsibilities. Relate your school experience to the skills or knowledge that you acquired, not to specific coursework. If you're switching fields, note similarities between your current or previous job and the job you seek.

Step 3: Instruct

You've grabbed the reader's attention. You've detailed your support points. Now tell your reader how to take advantage of the offer you've made or the advantages you've promised. After all, if you're going to participate in the hiring process, you've got to tell your reader how to reach you.

Generally, this can be handled quickly and simply. This is not to suggest, however, that this part of your letter is unimportant. On the contrary, *instructing* is all too often overlooked or rushed through by job-hunters... and it's a shame. This step is as important as your opening. Why? Because the likelihood that your correspondence will achieve the response you desire increases with each additional line that your reader reads. So if your reader is still with you at this point in your letter, chances are she's interested in you. Therefore, you want to get to her while her interest level is high. What's more, the simpler it is for her to take the next step, the greater the chance is that she will take the step. Therefore, you want to make your instructions easy to understand, and even easier to follow.

To get the reader to respond to your letter, you've got to *tell the reader what to do*, and be specific. Provide appropriate and complete contact information so that the reader can select a preferred method of communicating. Indicate your work, home, and/or mobile phone numbers and give your e-mail address, then state which of these is best for reaching you and when. If confidentiality is an issue, ask your reader to maintain it when calling.

If the next step is going to be *yours*, you've got to *tell the reader what to expect*. Be equally specific about what you will do. Say when you'll follow up. Say how you'll follow up: by phone or by e-mail. Tell the reader what information you've attached, if any. If you'll be sending additional material, say when it will arrive.

Finally, the hiring process will stop dead in its tracks if you don't follow up the way you promised. So do it.

You'll find examples of this vital step in virtually every sample letter in this book. Here are just a few.

RECRUITER'S TIP ⟩ **Don't Play Hard to Get!**

A strong letter can make your reader want to contact you immediately. Don't miss this opportunity! Always position your phone number(s) and e-mail address so that the reader can't miss them. Place them:

- Prominently at the top of each page of your resume.
- As part of the masthead of your resume and the matching letterhead on your cover letter if you attach it as a .pdf.
- In the body of your letter or e-mail.
- Under your name and signature.

Samples of instructing.

- I look forward to hearing from you and have included my e-mail address and phone numbers.

- I will wait to hear from you. My direct line at work is (555) 765-4321, or you may call me at home at (555) 456-7890.
- I will await your response. You may reach me at home (555) 456-7890) or via e-mail at marybrown@zmail.com.
- I hope you will contact me in the very near future. I am anxious to discuss the possibility of our working together. You'll find my address and telephone numbers below.
- Because my current employer is unaware of my job search, I would appreciate it if you could contact me at home during the evenings at (555) 456-7890 or by e-mail at marybrown@zmail.com.
- Please feel free to call me evenings at my home or to leave a voice message. My home number is (555) 456-7890. (My present employer is unaware of my job search.)
- I'll contact your office shortly to see when we might meet.
- I'll call your assistant on Wednesday of next week to set up a meeting.
- I'll be in town throughout the month of December, and will contact you to schedule an appointment.
- I'll give you a call on the 18th of this month to set up a meeting. In the meantime, please feel free to contact me at (555) 765-4321.
- I will send my references first thing tomorrow morning. If there is anything else you need, please let me know. You can reach me or leave a message on my cell phone: (555) 765-4321.

Optional Step 4: Close Warmly

Unless your correspondence is extremely strong and hard-hitting, you should generally add a final line at the end. You might thank the reader for taking the time to read your letter or for considering you as a candidate.

The following sample closings will help you out in a variety of job-hunting situations, as will the many examples contained in the sample letters throughout this book.

Sample closings.

- I look forward to hearing from you.
- I look forward to meeting with you at your earliest convenience.
- I thank you for your consideration.
- Thank you for your interest.

- I would welcome the opportunity to work with you.
- I would welcome the opportunity to contribute my skills to your organization/firm/team, and look forward to speaking with you soon.
- I'd like to put my expertise to work for you.
- I'd be pleased to demonstrate my abilities firsthand.

How to Respond to Salary Queries

Ads and job postings often ask for information about your current salary or salary history. Should you reveal it? What you should not do is ignore the question. Prospective employers may assume that your salary requirements are either too high to be realistic or too low to admit. They may assume that you feel above answering their queries, or that you are less than thorough in your efforts. If they assume any one of these things, you're out of luck. Some online applications may not even allow you to submit without completing this field.

How should you handle this challenging issue? When you must include a figure, use the Internet to research salary ranges. Some sites provide average salaries for specific countries, regions, U.S. states, and even cities. Use this information as a baseline, then adjust it up or down to reflect your age, education, experience level, and other factors that may be relevant to your situation. If appropriate, include the dollar equivalent of benefits and/or job perks, such as a company car or an expense account.

When a definite figure is not demanded, another strategy is that used by the author of Letter 5-1, written in response to an ad in a trade publication that read, "Serious candidates will provide salary history."

This writer knew that the ad would generate a great deal of interest and produce a multitude of responses. He also realized that the employer would be looking for ways to reduce the number of candidates to a reasonable size, such as rejecting those who ignored the request for a dollar figure, rejecting those whose salary history was too low to indicate a sufficient degree of authority in past jobs, or rejecting those whose salary expectations were too high. He believed that stating a specific figure could eliminate him from consideration immediately. Furthermore, his primary goal in writing this cover letter was to secure an interview, during which he would have the opportunity to discuss benefits, perks, and other issues affecting salary. As you'll see in the final paragraph of his letter, he effectively shapes a deal with his reader: if you give me what I want (an interview), I'll give you what you want (a salary discussion). In this way, he has not avoided the question of salary. Instead, he has used it to his advantage. In fact, he was selected to be interviewed.

There are other options as well. You may simply state that salary is a negotiable issue for you, one that you will be happy to explore in an interview. If you feel compelled to include a dollar figure, you may prefer to give a broad salary range or state an amount that reflects your total compensation (some combination of salary, bonus, anticipated raise, incentives, benefits, and perks such as a car, expense accounts, and club memberships). Your industry may dictate the way in which you will calculate such a figure. For instance, someone who works only three days each week might calculate what her salary would be if she worked five days. A teacher might calculate what his annual salary would be if he earned it for 12 months rather than the 9 he actually teaches. Whatever you decide, be sure you can substantiate it during the interview.

LETTER 5-1 ▸ Marketing Communications Supervisor—Salary

I am applying for the position of Marketing Communications Supervisor because your ad said these three things to me:

- Your eloquent description of how the position fulfills the corporate mission set it apart from all the other ads on the staffUP website and "beat the clutter," the dream of all retailers.
- Your description of the ideal candidate reflects <u>my</u> skills, <u>my</u> strengths, and <u>my</u> experience.
- You are a substantive company offering a product of superior quality.

My resume, which is attached, speaks of my experience and expertise in retailing, and most recently in the marketing of organic specialty foods. I am assertive, diligent, driven, and hardworking. I am a seeker of end results—and I achieve them, as the many accomplishments listed on my resume prove. I thrive <u>and deliver</u> in a demanding and fast-paced environment. I am willing to tackle any project. My management style is open, humorous, example-driven, and loyal.

Sells personal strengths.

I believe that we can be successful partners. I want the chance to meet with you and would consider an interview a wonderful opportunity. I'll make myself available at your convenience so that we may discuss salary in detail, and I can provide references.

I look forward to hearing from you.

Samples

The following pages contain samples of well-written Ad Response and Resume Cover Letters. Peruse these samples to find ideas that appeal to you or inspire you as you create your own "killer" letters. As you do, keep in mind the following important points:

Summarize. Generalize. Customize. The letters included here represent a variety of industries and positions. Nevertheless, you'll discover that our writers have summarized, generalized, and customized so effectively that many letters would work equally well in other fields. Don't be surprised that you don't find endless details, facts, and dates—all that is resume material! These letters focus less on listing specific experiences and more on providing an overview of those experiences and an interpretation of the benefits that such experiences offer a potential employer. Your letters should do the same.

You Can't Argue With Success. Past achievements can indicate future success, so be sure to include examples of your most impressive accomplishments. Use bullets or numbers instead of embedding them in the middle of a paragraph so that they won't be overlooked even by those who skim.

Copy, customize, and send these letters and e-mails . . . it's perfectly legal! When you bought this book, you purchased the right to copy and adapt the letters in it. By all means, use the samples provided here, although you may wish to adapt them in case your interviewer or your competition uses the same letter. *This link will connect you to all the letters online:* http://www.mh professional.com/mediacenter.

This and the next few letters are ideal for those who like to get right to the point.

LETTER 5-2 Ad Response Letter—General

I urge you not to hire anyone until we've met. That's because I possess every one of the seven qualifications you list in your ad—and more—as the attached resume reveals.

The sooner we meet, the sooner I can begin producing results for you, your team, and your company. Why not give me a call at (555) 456-7890 during the day or evening? I will be pleased to meet with you at your convenience.

Let's get together!

LETTER 5-3 Ad Response Letter—General

The hiring process is tough enough without interviewing countless candidates who responded to your listing despite being underqualified or overqualified. I can save you from this onerous, time-consuming task.

As my resume indicates, I possess every one of the qualifications you seek, and I am available to meet with you at once and begin working right away.

Why not give me a call and streamline what might otherwise be a lengthy interview process? I look forward to hearing from you.

LETTER 5-4 ▸ **Ad Response Letter—General**

With responsibilities and deadlines that won't wait, why spend valuable time interviewing unqualified candidates?

As you'll see from the enclosed resume, I have the educational background, professional experience, and track record for which you are searching. In addition, I am motivated and enthusiastic, and would appreciate the opportunity to contribute to your firm's success.

I can promise that meeting with me will not be a waste of your time—and I will make myself available at your convenience, during or outside of normal business hours.

Sincerely,

LETTER 5-5 ▸ **Ad Response Letter—General**

Dear Mr. Hiring:

An innovative company like yours thrives because it hires innovative thinkers like me!

Over the years, I have developed a reputation for introducing fresh approaches to solve the challenges faced in today's competitive business world. Because this is a personality trait—not a learned skill—it is something that I can offer your firm with confidence. It is who I am. It has defined the contributions I have made in every position I have held.

My resume, which is attached, begins to tell my story. A personal meeting with you will supply vivid details. The references I'll provide will support them.

Please call me at (555) 456-7890 to schedule an interview. I promise you won't be disappointed.

LETTER 5-6 ▸ Ad Response Letter—General

The educational background, experience, and skills listed in your advertisement are only the beginning of what I can bring to your firm.

As you'll see in the outline of accomplishments I've included with this letter, I have a solid history of producing results within a limited budget. I have built and successfully managed a staff of 20, and I deal effectively with customers, executives, and stockholders on a regular basis. All of these achievements are critical to firms such as yours that must compete in today's difficult economy.

My resume is attached as proof that I meet all the criteria listed in your ad. An interview would give me the chance to further prove my unique strengths.

I hope to hear from you shortly.

LETTER 5-7 ▸ Ad Response Letter—General

In today's challenging economic climate, many people will respond to your advertisement. Few will be interviewed. One will be hired.

However...

Of the many who will respond, few will be as qualified as I am, since I have 12 years of in-depth, bona fide industry experience. No one else will bring my track record and the expertise I can offer—expertise that equips me to start delivering results for you *immediately*. With minimal training. With minimal disruption. With maximum positive effect on your bottom line.

I will make myself available to meet with you at your convenience. Thank you for your consideration.

This is a gutsy approach, balanced by the tactful reference to "unavoidable cost cutting" and supported by solid, relevant experience.

LETTER 5-8   Ad Response Letter—General—Job Loss

Dear Ms. Ovett:

Because I have long admired your achievement in building a successful company, I was dismayed to learn of your recent layoffs. In today's economy, such a situation presents the vexing conundrum: how to maximize opportunities for growth with diminished human resources?

> Opening identifies a need.

Optimizing the resources you can employ is, of course, a viable solution—one that I can offer if you will grant me the chance to meet with you.

When we meet, you'll find me to be a person with a positive outlook who enjoys identifying ways to make something work rather than looking for reasons not to try. This perspective is invaluable in setting an example for employees who are called upon to assume numerous responsibilities—of particular merit in this era of unavoidable downsizing and cost cutting.

In addition, my resume illustrates that I possess the background and experience that our industry demands and your success deserves.

Ms. Ovett, if I have taken great liberty in writing to you, it is because I firmly believe that I can contribute to your firm's continued expansion. I will call you early next week to see whether we might get together.

Sincerely,

LETTER 5-9 Ad Response—General—Student

Good opening
when the ad
does not provide
a name.

To the Director of Human Resources:

After four years in college, what have I learned? Plenty! Plenty that I can apply directly to the entry-level position listed on your website's Career Center.

The drive to focus and achieve. Your firm's success depends upon the ability of your staff to grasp a problem, evaluate the best way to solve it, and then work until the solution is in hand. This is precisely the process I followed during all four years to graduate with a 3.80 average.

Flexibility and creativity. A business gets stale when it recycles the same ideas time and time again. When you hire me, you get someone who thinks for himself, and who is not afraid to suggest new ways to approach a task, as I did as the Student Representative responsible for researching and updating State University's ethical standards to reflect the difficult issues facing today's students and faculty.

The ability to work with a diverse population. Having been raised in a multiethnic environment and educated in a multi-cultural institution, and with a degree in psychology, I am well equipped to interact productively with customers and staff from a variety of backgrounds and with a range of priorities, from intern to senior leadership.

An interview would give me the opportunity to demonstrate my abilities. I will call you soon to see if we might meet. Or you can reach me at the number listed below.

Thank you in advance for considering me.

LETTER 5-10   General—Language Skills

To the Placement Experts at Idiom International:

With my fluency in Mandarin, English, and Spanish, I can help businesses operating in today's global marketplace acquire a broader customer base as they enhance their international brand.

With my in-depth experience in the travel and entertainment industry (as detailed on the attached resume), I can offer these firms the opportunity to serve more customers, from more cultures, more personally, and more appropriately than ever before.

With your strength in worldwide placement, you can help us both profit by successfully matching my rare qualifications with the needs of a growing firm.

I will call you Monday to see if we might schedule an appointment. I look forward to meeting you personally.

Until then,

> Great line when responding to a P.O. box.

LETTER 5-11 ▸ General—Jobhopper—Salary

I appreciate your willingness to assist in my job search. As promised, I have attached my resume to provide background on my professional experience. To bring my resume to life for you, allow me to tell you more about myself and what sets me apart from other candidates.

Turns a negative into a positive.

Over the years, I have performed in a variety of environments. As a result, I have been exposed to diverse people, work styles, standards of measurement, corporate cultures, and demands. What has remained consistent throughout is my ability to produce results in a range of business climates.

I have contributed to the success of management teams and worked on my own without supervision. I have mastered the ability to deal with frustrated customers, management under pressure, and companies operating in the midst of labor negotiations and layoffs. Throughout, I have received consistently high praise from superiors and coworkers, many of whom are ready to serve as references, should you wish to contact them.

Enhances credibility.

To an employer, I present a positive, results-oriented work ethic, and a professional, pleasant demeanor. To you, I present a strong, solid candidate with a willingness to remain flexible in terms of salary requirements.

I will contact you next week to continue our discussion and to solicit any advice you may offer in my search. I thank you again for any help you can provide.

How should you respond when an entry-level position is barely described or the company is not named? This letter and the ones that follow provide some answers.

LETTER 5-12   Entry Level—Student

To the Director of Human Resources:

Your ad for an entry-level position caught my attention as I prepare to begin my professional career upon graduation this spring from State University.

I write "professional" career because I have worked steadily throughout college, gaining valuable experience that equips me to present your firm with advantages others may not offer.

For example, as a Resident Assistant for a 250-person coed dormitory, I acquired strong leadership and interpersonal skills. I am now able to think quickly on my feet in emergency situations, and in those requiring quick assessment of many factors in order to make appropriate decisions. Dealing with the diverse concerns of students, parents, and faculty, I have become adept at operating with the proper mix of authority, diplomacy, and tact.

While working in this demanding position, I achieved a 3.75 cumulative grade point average. My double major, Communications and Political Science, provided me with a thorough foundation in principles that affect businesses every day.

> Translates life experience to employers' needs.

I would welcome the chance to discuss openings at your firm. If you will contact me at (555) 456-7890, we can schedule a meeting.

Thank you for your consideration.

LETTER 5-13   Entry Level—Student

To the Director of Human Resources:

Attached to this note is my resume, which details my education, work experience, and technical proficiency—all important criteria in your search to fill the entry-level position advertised.

<u>Allow me to introduce the person with whom you and your colleagues will work, should you choose to interview and hire me.</u>

I possess strong moral and ethical principles, which led me to put in long, hard hours at school and part-time jobs in order to succeed in a challenging educational environment. These values also motivate me to perform diligently and loyally to contribute to my employer's profitability. Unlike others, I do not expect to begin as a vice president. I know that it takes commitment, dedication, and intelligence to rise within a firm, all of which I offer you.

As one of six children, I also have an active sense of humor, which has been useful in defusing difficult situations. I have the patience to see an assignment through to completion. I am comfortable delivering presentations to a group, working as part of a team, and helping others succeed.

It would be an honor to meet with you personally to discover more about the opening at your firm and how I can assist your organization in its growth. Please contact me at the address or phone number listed above. I will make myself available at your convenience.

Thank you.

LETTER 5-14   Entry Level—Student

To the Director of Human Resources:

For the entry-level opening at your firm, why not consider someone like me with a strong academic background and real-world business experience? As you'll see on the enclosed resume, I have recently completed my undergraduate studies at State University. My perseverance and consistent effort enabled me to maintain my Dean's List status while working on a part-time basis.

Rather than work at a mindless job that might pay the bills but would teach me little of practical value, I chose to open and operate my own painting company. I selected and trained crew members, developed an advertising program, borrowed the money to cover start-up costs (which was repaid in full after just six months), and handled scheduling, payroll, and tax reporting. Over the four years I've been running my business, I have served more than 80 different customers, 54 of whom have called back to schedule additional jobs.

My experience has prepared me to meet the demands of the business world, and I am anxious to apply my strengths and talents in the corporate environment. I would appreciate the opportunity to meet with you to explore this possibility.

Thank you for considering me.

LETTER 5-15   Entry Level—Student—Sales

The background and experience I can offer in reply to your posting for an entry-level sales position may prove ideal for your needs. Allow me to introduce myself and my qualifications.

This June, I will receive my Bachelor of Science in Psychology from State University. In addition to my rigorous course study, I participated in extracurricular activities that provided me with the hands-on experience that is so vital to being a successful sales representative.

As Rush Chairman for my fraternity, I planned and directed a major program to introduce the strengths that our product delivered and promote them in a market that was rife with competition. Through these efforts, we have enjoyed an <u>increase in membership of 20% over the past three years</u>. I further developed and managed a program to raise funds for our nonaffiliated charity, the Brothers of Hope. Targeting fraternity members, students at large, faculty, and the community, program <u>contributions exceeded previous years' totals by 77%</u>.

To achieve these goals, I combined an ability to plan, to visualize solutions creatively, and to implement them successfully with my talent in dealing with people. These are the same characteristics I would bring to your organization.

Please consider me a serious candidate for your sales position. I will be happy to visit your offices for an interview. I can be reached at the telephone numbers printed below.

Sincerely,

LETTER 5-16   Entry Level—Student

To the Director of Human Resources:

When my mother and father sent me from our village in China to America, I was fortunate to live with relatives who encouraged me to excel—and I have. I quickly mastered English and a new culture, and I achieved and maintained a 3.50 average at State University.

When I was granted a full scholarship, I was fortunate to have the time to devote to volunteer work in addition to my studies. I served for four years on the university's Community Relations Board as a liaison between the school, neighboring politicians, residents, and businesses. This valuable experience prepared me to deal effectively with consumers, business clients, shareholders, coworkers, and executives at every level of management.

When I graduate this May, I will be fortunate once again if I have secured employment with a firm such as yours. My ability to work productively with others, my drive to excel, and my unique cultural perspective equip me to become a valuable member of your organization.

I hope you will contact me to arrange an interview so that I can provide you with additional information to supplement what appears on my resume. I look forward to hearing from you.

Sincerely,

LETTER 5-17   Entry Level—Student

This past May, I graduated from State University magna cum laude with a 3.80 average, having financed 100% of my college education myself. As you can see, I am not afraid of hard work and would welcome the chance to discuss with you the entry-level opening at your firm.

My resume describes my academic background and professional experience. As you'll see, my four years of solid work experience exposed me to substantial interaction with consumers. I consider myself skilled in dealing with the public, and I would prove a positive representative for your firm.

Working summers on the alumni newsletter, I learned to coordinate an inordinate number of facts, figures, dates, and details—under deadline pressure!

These skills, combined with the drive to work through difficulty toward the successful completion of a project, will make me a productive addition to your organization. I look forward to the opportunity to meet.

Sincerely,

LETTER 5-18   Training Program—Student—Referral Letter

Your associate, Amy Levin, advised me that she had forwarded my resume to you for consideration as a 20XX participant in Morgan Stanley's training program. I have attached another copy for your convenience.

On May 25, I will graduate from State University with a major in Economics, a minor in Business Administration, and a concentration in Mathematics. I am planning a career in investment banking, for which my education has ideally prepared me.

Ms. Levin and others have spoken highly of your firm's training program. It is precisely the type of challenge I am seeking. In return, I offer Morgan Stanley a loyal and hardworking employee who already possesses a solid foundation of relevant knowledge. Unlike other applicants, who may have had more general studies, my education would allow me to be a highly productive member of your training program. As an investment banker, I would be able to put this supplemental training to profitable use more quickly for the institution.

I would appreciate the opportunity to meet with you. I can be in New York any Friday this semester, or any day after graduation.

I look forward to hearing from you and thank you for your consideration.

LETTER 5-19   Customer Representative—Student

Appropriate
salutation when
the ad bears
no name.

To the Vice President:

As a State University senior who will be graduating in May of 20XX, I am submitting this application because I believe I can offer your firm an unusual mix of abilities, talents, and enthusiasm.

For instance:

- My double major (Economics/English Literature) demonstrates my willingness to assume more than the typical level of responsibility and to achieve in a challenging environment.

- Through my coursework, I acquired in-depth technical proficiency and a profound belief in the importance of effective communication for today's growing entrepreneurial endeavor.

- To finance my education, I planned, launched, and operated a highly successful catering business. I gained hands-on experience in properly managing revenues, time, and employees.

As you can see, I am goal-oriented, driven, and not afraid of hard work—qualifications that are vital for anyone who will be a productive staff member for your firm, as I would like to be.

I look forward to hearing from you so that we may schedule an interview.

LETTER 5-20   Entry-Level Paralegal—Career Change

What a wonderful service you provide! Placing qualified professionals within the legal profession serves the needs of many, particularly someone like myself who is entering the field with so much to offer.

As I near completion of the ABA-approved Paralegal Program at State College, I am preparing to offer my skills to Los Angeles County law firms. In addition to my superior, straight-A record in this program, I have a background in the business world that arms me with a valuable perspective that others may not have.

For 20 years, I was an integral member of Digital Electronics' product innovation team. In this capacity, I worked closely with federal regulators and patent attorneys, and I can bring this experience to bear on behalf of your clients.

Also, I am trained in automated legal research programs (LexisNexis and Westlaw), and maintain my student password.

I would welcome the chance to pursue any openings for which you feel I may be qualified.

LETTER 5-21   Entry-Level Paralegal—Part-Time/Full-Time

RE: Entry-Level Paralegal Position

An entry-level position is not de facto fillable only by the inexperienced. On the contrary, in me you have a talented professional who is available for full- or part-time work.

Having performed in a range of capacities in law firms both large and small, as the attached resume reveals, I can offer you a wealth of legal capabilities, including:

- Contract preparation, negotiation, and administration in support of legal counsel.

- Ability to serve as an independent contract paralegal and investigator, as I have for many different attorneys and firms in the metropolitan area.

- Comprehensive paralegal skills, obtained through practical experience as well as in study leading to Paralegal Certification at State College.

I would appreciate the opportunity to interview with you and can make myself available at your convenience.

I thank you in advance for your consideration.

LETTER 5-22 Paralegal—Relocation

Dear Ms. Moore:

This August I will be relocating to Atlanta, where I hope to continue serving as a paralegal. My work with first-rate attorneys equips me to offer you an exceptional mix of training, knowledge, experience, and professionalism.

As you'll see on the enclosed resume, I have worked for several law firms in the Philadelphia area. I am proficient in many areas of criminal and civil trials, with an additional concentration in contracts and titles. As a result, I can offer you an unusual level of expertise in researching complaints and discovery requests as well as responses to counterclaims, motions for discovery sanctions, motions for summary judgments, and motions to dismiss.

The attorneys with whom I work have provided me with superior recommendations to aid me in my search. I would appreciate the opportunity to present these to you, and to introduce myself as a candidate for the position at your firm.

Supports candidacy.

I will be in Atlanta at the end of this month. If you will contact me at (555) 765-4321 during the day or evening, we can schedule an appointment.

Thank you.

LETTER 5-23   Administrative Assistant—Language Skills

Voilà! You've found the administrative assistant you're looking for in me.

I have all the qualifications listed in your ad . . . and more! My experience is relevant and extensive, as described in the attached resume. My typing has been called "lightning quick," and I am fluent in both PC and Mac office programs.

Brings her to life!

What my resume cannot illustrate is <u>what sets me apart from other candidates</u>—namely, my penchant for organization, my eye for detail, my positive and personable nature, and my ability to perform, even in the pressure-cooker environment of a fast-paced, fast-growing global firm.

Furthermore, I am fluent in Spanish and have fair skill in Arabic, having been raised in a multicultural family. These language abilities will help you in dealing with international customers and prospects, as will my familiarity with foreign customs and protocol.

I would be pleased to come in for a personal meeting. I will call you shortly to set up an appointment.

Gracias,

LETTER 5-24   Administrative Assistant—Workforce
                  Return—Career Change

RE: Your posting on Monster.com for an Assistant to the President

Dear Ms. Lockhart:

Impeccable interpersonal skills. Organizational and supervisory abilities. Attention to detail. Your ad describes my strengths precisely!

 <u>People Power.</u> As a teacher in the public school system for
 three years, I am adept at dealing with people—from "by the
 book" career administrators to the high school bully, from irate
 parents to the shy underachiever, from goal-oriented department heads to aggressive textbook and technology sales reps.

 <u>Management Skills.</u> As a homemaker raising two children, I
 mastered the ability to spearhead three projects simultaneously
 while supervising two distinct groups of youngsters, maintaining my patience and my good temper all the while.

 <u>Accuracy.</u> As a volunteer for a local hospital, I coordinated the
 ever-changing schedules of 50 unpaid workers for five years with
 nary a "mix-up."

Handling these responsibilities provided me with a <u>different kind of
experience</u>: the kind the corporate world just doesn't offer—and the
kind that proves invaluable once you enter this world, as I'd like to do
now.

I hope you'll consider me a serious candidate for the position of Assistant to the President. I certainly would take the job very seriously,
proving an asset to the president and to the company.

Sincerely,

While maintaining her professionalism, this candidate allows her sense of humor to shine through—a refreshing change from the many other letters the ad produced.

LETTER 5-25   Executive Secretary

Dear Ms. Hilman:

Thank you for advertising for an Executive Secretary to work with your top partners. Until I saw your advertisement, I thought no one would appreciate the unusual combination of skills I can offer!

My resume is attached; allow me to present the highlights here:

Superior PC and Mac abilities, including skills in Word, Power-Point, Excel, and Publisher, as well as...

...social media, including Facebook, Twitter, LinkedIn, Instagram, YouTube, and more through...

...four years at Disney and three years at a Miami-based law firm specializing in medical malpractice, which accounts for my...

...professionalism in dealing with the public, attorneys, physicians, emotional clients, and the media...

...as well as my experience in making travel arrangements for overworked lawyers who wish to escape all this!

As an administrative assistant at a smaller firm, I am anxious to assume the additional responsibilities described in your job posting. I hope you will contact me for an interview; my contact information appears below. Thank you in advance.

Sincerely,

LETTER 5-26 ▸ Office Administrator—Salary—Language

To meet the extensive qualifications listed on your website's Careers page, a candidate must be a true professional with in-depth experience at a major corporation who is looking for an exciting new challenge, as I am.

For example, your ad requests:	and I deliver:
Experience screening telephone calls, responding, and routing accordingly	Two years as a receptionist for General American Products
Ability to order, maintain, and distribute office supply inventory	Seven years as Office Manager for IBN Executive Offices
Skill in scheduling and coordinating training, events, conferences, meetings, and on-site demos	Seven years doing the same, in addition to coordinating travel arrangements for 15 IBN executives

In addition, I possess a degree in Business Administration, exceptional interpersonal and written communication skills, and easy fluency in Spanish. I would be pleased to demonstrate my technical abilities when we meet and to also detail my salary history and requirements for you.

These qualifications, combined with my substantial experience, would make me a productive, effective Office Administrator from my first day on the job. I hope you'll contact me at my home number below; I look forward to meeting you.

LETTER 5-27 Consulting Associate—Recent MBA—Career Change

I am writing to explore the possibility of pursuing an associate's position at Doniger-Davis. Currently, I am a Relationship Officer at American First Bancorporation, where I handle the financial accounts of high-net-worth individuals. In May of 20XX, I will earn my MBA in Finance from State University.

My interest in management consulting has been piqued by specific and fascinating classes that are part of the MBA program. Business Policy, Strategic Implementation, and Managing Human Systems, in particular, demonstrated to me that my education, interpersonal talents, and practical experience would prove immensely productive in a consulting environment.

With five years in the financial services industry, I can offer your firm a specialty with broad application. My involvement with interviewing and assessing prospective employees and with quality-improvement projects may free you from the in-depth training that would be required for a less-experienced candidate.

I've attached a copy of my resume for your information. I will call next week to see when we might get together. In the meantime, I thank you for your consideration. I look forward to meeting you.

LETTER 5-28 Consulting

I enjoyed speaking with you on the phone this afternoon and appreciate your interest.

As promised, I have enclosed my resume, which details my unusually thorough background in public relations, business communications, and human resources development. What my resume does not describe is my character. I am a conceptual thinker, a generator of creative ideas, and a self-starter.

I would welcome the opportunity to demonstrate these qualities in person and look forward to hearing from you.

Sincerely,

LETTER 5-29   Events Planner

Your advertisement for an Events Planner was of particular interest to me because I encounter so few organizations that recognize the unique value of special events. By relegating this function to already overworked marketing departments, where planning withers and presentation suffocates, most firms waste this vital opportunity.

Since SYTEX is not like most firms, and I am not like most Events Planners, perhaps we should meet.

I would like to discover more about your events schedule. And I would like to describe my experience designing, planning, preparing, promoting, and running annual meetings, companywide divisional meetings, regional breakfast meetings, trade shows, seminars, and webinars. I have planned and run many events that generated important new business potential while enhancing the firm's corporate image.

This past year, I also orchestrated a tour of the Greek islands for an elite client group that solidified key relationships.

Attached you'll find my resume, along with a description of programs I have designed and the results they have produced. It would be an honor to meet you in person and to be considered as a member of the SYTEX staff.

LETTER 5-30   Media Buyer—Social Media—Student

Thank you for taking the time to address us at State University's Media Day. Your energizing talk has piqued my interest in the Assistant Buyer position at BBDO Worldwide. I would not write to you without a firm conviction concerning the match between your needs and my analytical, communication, and organizational skills and my enthusiasm.

Allow me to highlight my qualifications for this position:

- Firsthand experience **thinking on my feet** and **reacting quickly and responsibly**. As an intern at Burson Marsteller, I single-handedly ran the student portion of a PR conference, including a last-minute improv when a speaker didn't show up!

- Forged-in-the-fire **communication skills**, honed through working events and sweepstakes at Fallon Worldwide. In this role, I mastered the dreaded "cold call," persuading organizers to let my clients attend these tightly controlled events.

- Tried and tested **planning and organizing abilities**, developed by managing experimental events for diverse clients. I learned the ropes quickly, took control, got organized, and stayed that way throughout each project. Although it was a challenge, I enjoyed the fast-paced environment and the responsibility.

I believe that these skills are vital to the successful BBDO Worldwide Assistant Buyer. What's more, I would welcome involvement in digital media buying, including interactive display and video and social, mobile, and other rich media.

I'd be thrilled to have the opportunity to interview with you in person or connect by phone to discuss future opportunities with BBDO Worldwide. Please feel free to reach me by phone at (123) 456-7890 or via e-mail. I look forward to hearing from you. Thank you very much for your time and consideration.

LETTER 5-31 Art Director

Having researched your agency and the exceptional results your teams produce, I know your firm values creative talent and hard work—both of which I can deliver.

From among the hundreds of resumes you receive from people seeking a position with your agency, I urge you to consider mine because my skill set differs from those of other graphic designers. For example:

- As a seasoned Art Director/Graphic Designer, I possess extensive corporate experience, having worked with many of today's leading firms: Yahoo!, Verizon, Bank of America, Apple, and FedEx, among others.

- With more than 9+ years of digital advertising experience, I stay resolutely up to date on the latest technologies, currently Photoshop, Illustrator, ImageReady, and Flash 9. I have also worked directly with code and possess a thorough grasp of front-end languages such as HTML, CSS, and JavaScript.

- I partner effectively with creative, content, and account teams, as well as with developers, clients, and management, and I thrive in a deadline-driven, cross-functional team environment.

With my unique combination of qualifications, you can welcome to your agency a genuine creative talent and true professional—just as I would welcome the opportunity to meet with you.

LETTER 5-32 Copywriter

GOOD NEWS!

There is a copywriter only a phone call away who knows the difference between a CDO, an LBO, and EFTs ... one who can express complex details clearly and convincingly to consumers, investors, and shareholders.

I am an experienced advertising copywriter with a strong financial services orientation—and the time to put this expertise to work for UniFirst!

With me, you'll add an exceptional member to your marketing team; I've created pitchbooks and proposals, website content, print ads, banners and exhibit booths, newsletters, blog posts, and corporate identity pieces. And unlike most writers, my background includes staff positions with both advertising agencies and banks. What this means for you is that you'll save hours negotiating with legal counsel, thanks to my in-depth knowledge of government regulations such as Dodd-Frank, the Volcker Rule, and restrictions on financial advertising. My in-depth experience in the financial services industry means that I will be productive immediately without wasting your resources and time on training.

Can I tell you more? If so, you may reach me via e-mail or at (555) 765-4321. Thank you in advance for your consideration.

LETTER 5-33   Senior Marketing Communications
Officer—Social Media

**RE: TheLadders.com post for a Senior Marketing
Communications Officer**

It takes more than an understanding of new media to be effective in
today's rapidly evolving and highly competitive marketing arena. It
takes a record of <u>success</u> in deploying each new technology, application, and innovation . . . *precisely what I can deliver.*

Through the strategic integration of multimedia marketing, advertising, and public relations tactics, I have repeatedly boosted market
share and catapulted revenue, visibility, and brand loyalty for agency
clients. What's more, I possess special expertise in:

- Online media planning and placement
- Interactive content development
- Website development
- Social media campaigns

My resume, which is attached, details the results I've produced for a
diverse and demanding clientele. I would welcome the chance to meet
and discuss in depth how this expertise can help you drive your organization's and your clients' continued growth and success.

LETTER 5-34 Account Executive—Salary

Your advertisement caught my eye immediately, as it describes a position for which my qualifications are ideal.

My solid experience in sales, marketing, and cultivating relationships with both prospects and clients enables you to add a proven professional to your team—one who can begin being productive at once. Allow me to highlight my strengths:

- Nearly five years of success selling high-tech, high-touch equipment to national corporate accounts.

- Highly effective presentation skills with which I influence decision makers and then train them in the use of the new technology.

- In-depth experience developing and sharing marketing strategies and techniques with fellow team members.

- Comfort working on a salary-plus-commission basis.

My resume provides full details on my background and accomplishments. Realizing that these data cannot adequately convey my personal strengths, I would appreciate the opportunity to meet with you and discuss salary in greater depth, as requested. Thank you for your consideration.

LETTER 5-35 ▸ Product Manager

If you're looking for an exceptional Product Manager with insight, creativity, a proven record in manufacturing and management, and an impressive work ethic, look no further.

Through hands-on experience at all levels of warehousing, production, and sales (detailed in the attached resume), I have developed superior analytical and interpersonal skills, marketing expertise, and a perspective and sophistication unique in our industry—all of which I can put to work for you.

I produce an endless supply of new ideas. I can generate solutions to problems where none seem possible. And I will teach, inspire, and motivate others to do the same.

I look forward to speaking with you soon to set up a convenient time for us to meet. I can be reached at (555) 765-4321 during the day or evening.

LETTER 5-36   Product Design/Development—Social Media

The contributions I have made on behalf of my current employer preview what I can offer Millman Clothing. As Associate Product Developer in Extreme Sport Activewear, I:

- Developed an innovative extreme performance mountaineering line and directed a social media campaign that "went viral," catapulting sales to $3M in the first two months.

- Have complete responsibility for managing all National Sales sample lines, forecasting demand and production levels.

- **Initiate, maintain, and manage key relationships** with global manufacturing firms.

- Research market, consumer, and competitive trends in order to identify **revenue-generating product merchandising opportunities**.

As you'll see on my resume, in each of my roles, I have had a direct and positive impact on the company's bottom-line profitability—and I can do the same for Millman. May we have the chance to meet and explore this promising opportunity in greater detail?

LETTER 5-37   Cruise Product Development—Career Change

If you are searching for a creative thinker with extensive experience selling to both companies and individuals, we should meet.

As Senior Manager of Sales and Marketing at the Ames Company, I am eager to transfer my skills from manufacturing to the travel industry.

- Through delightful cruises in the Caribbean, the Mediterranean, Alaska, and South America, <u>I have become familiar with (and a fan of) the many superb benefits</u> that cruising offers individuals, groups, and corporate planners.

- Through my business travel throughout Asia and Europe, <u>I know firsthand the business-building and revenue-generating opportunity such programs deliver.</u> .

- Through my work with a diverse client base, <u>I have become extremely proficient in promoting high-ticket items</u> by identifying and focusing on the advantages they offer to a diverse constituency.

Because I am currently seeking to broaden my horizons—literally and figuratively—I await your reply so that we can arrange a personal meeting. Then, we can discuss how my particular blend of capabilities, experience, and managerial strengths can help your firm capture lucrative business opportunities.

This research professional is letting her work speak for her. She's also asked for advice on a resume—a good way to get it read more carefully.

LETTER 5-38   Market Research

Dear Mr. Green:

We spoke on Wednesday afternoon, and, as promised, I'm attaching a copy of my resume. Since it has been *ages* since I've circulated one, I would welcome any suggestions or advice.

I'm also enclosing copies of:

- Comparative market analyses of male fine apparel purchasers in New York and Chicago, which I conducted for a French clothing retailer.

- A report I compiled for a hydroponic produce farm exploring the efficacy of tapping markets in colder climates.

- A proposal for a focus group to help a major airline assess public reaction to a merger and scalebacks in its frequent-flyer program.

I welcome any guidance you may be willing to offer; thank you in advance.

With appreciation,

LETTER 5-39   Marketing/Branding—Product Management

RE: Opportunities in Product Management

Dear Ms. Crain:

Good opening in
letter to recruiter.

Your work and reputation within the branding/advertising/marketing industry suggest that you continually search for highly qualified executives to fill positions on both the agency and the client side.

For this reason, I am writing to introduce myself: a marketer who has spent the last 10 years promoting consumer and B2B initiatives. My work at Holmes & Richards equipped me with skills essential to the successful product manager: the ability to master complex product details and competitive positioning quickly, and the perspective to create, align, and communicate brand messages to cultivate trust among distinct, diverse market sectors.

These qualities are integral to the product manager who can build sales and profits for her agency and its client. In your clients' searches for managers to champion their companies' products, why not recommend a proven marketing expert, as I am? I would welcome the opportunity to meet you. I thank you in advance for your consideration.

LETTER 5-40 **Marketing Representative**

Dear Ms. DeMario and Mr. Williams:

Welcome to Baltimore!

With nontraditional marketing avenues rapidly expanding, these promise to be exciting times for those who are prepared to identify and creatively exploit new opportunities in new markets... as DeMario & Williams does. And as I do.

Attached is my resume and more: the profile of a successful marketer who has produced **tens of millions** of dollars over the last four years... who has **expertise in pharmaceuticals and neutriceuticals as well as mobile hardware, software, and apps**... who has **developed** business where none appeared to exist... who is **creative, self-motivated**, and **hungry** for a new challenge.

Because I've worked in New York, Philadelphia, and Baltimore (my hometown), I can offer DeMario & Williams an intimate perspective on the region's culture, persona, key players, and community leaders.

I would welcome the opportunity to demonstrate my strengths and talents in person and look forward to hearing from you.

LETTER 5-41 › Senior Marketing Associate

To the Director of Human Resources:

Timely opening.

Happy New Year! Throughout my eight years in marketing, the start of a new year invariably produced fresh ideas and renewed excitement for launching marketing initiatives—and now I can offer your firm a new perspective, as well.

The unprecedented volatility of the financial services industry has exposed me to a range of promotional challenges previously unknown in banking. I mastered the ability to identify and quantify objectives, refine them in response to market research, and develop detailed plans and budgets. I learned to think in entirely new ways, to motivate creative talent and produce campaigns, promotions, and individual sales pieces that added significantly to my employer's bottom line.

These are the skills that define the successful Senior Marketing Associate in any industry. I offer them to your firm—along with my in-depth experience in strategic planning for retail, commercial, and B2B advertising.

I look forward to hearing from you.

LETTER 5-42 ▸ Senior National Sales Consultant—IT—Salary

As the current top biller for a leading information technology company, I am writing to you because I am eager to expand from a regional sales territory to the national level—and can deliver several advantages that my peers may not offer you.

Promises benefits right up front.

Eight years selling computer hardware, software, electronics, Internet, and telecom equipment have equipped me with the following unique capabilities:

- Exceptional talent in strategy development and implementation.

- Proven strength in cultivating key account relationships to maximize opportunities for revenue growth.

- Recognized ability to work effectively on an independent basis without costly, time-consuming supervision.

- Strong presentation and sales closing skills that I can put to work immediately.

My resume, which is attached, details my career, accomplishments, and education (BA in Engineering/MBA). Currently, my total compensation is in the low six figures, including base salary, commissions, bonuses, and expenses. I would be pleased to discuss my qualifications and salary/commission requirements in greater detail when we meet in person.

If you would kindly contact me by phone at (555) 456-7890 or e-mail, I will make myself available at your convenience.

This writer's impressive accomplishments warrant a lengthy letter.

LETTER 5-43   Director—Corporate Marketing

With the financial services industry under pressure as never before, there is no time to waste in your search for a Director of Corporate Marketing. So I won't waste yours.

I am a Strategic Marketing Planning/Program Manager with 20+ years' experience, most recently in the telecom industry, and prior to that, in international transportation.

As head of Verizon's Marketing Services, I function as an internal Marketing Consultant to the organization's strategic business units, managing a staff of 14 marketing professionals and a $45M annual marketing budget, coordinating all advertising, research, branding, and public relations initiatives.

Marketing program improvements that I introduced doubled organizational visibility while slashing marketing expenses by 30%.

The success of my marketing programs during the last dozen years is directly attributable to several unique talents I can offer Boston First, including my abilities to:

- Leverage strategic planning skills to convert management's business plans into achievable, measureable marketing initiatives.
- Maximize my financial-controls experience to ensure that those same marketing programs are firmly grounded in economic reality.
- Creatively empower team members with increasing management responsibilities.
- Guarantee, through dedicated adherence to a TQM process, that all marketing programs are completed <u>on time, within budget, to the satisfaction of senior leadership</u>.

These are the proven achievements and talents I can bring to Boston First. Let's get together to discuss this opportunity in greater detail. I can be reached at (555) 456-7890.

LETTER 5-44   Director of Development
(Fund-Raising)—Career Change

$500 million is not the most—it's the <u>average</u> amount of money my fund-raising programs have generated for hospitals, private secondary schools, government programs, colleges, and universities.

> Killer opening!

This figure, attained through 22 years of intense fund-raising experience, equips me to assume the Director of Development responsibilities as rapidly and effectively as your needs demand.

I have attached summaries of my background and those projects that are most germane to your circumstances and setting. As you'll see, I have regularly built coalitions of citizens, alumni, and business and community leaders with the power to make significant contributions and to attract major funding from others.

My success at the Broderick Group has been enormously gratifying. However, I am eager to sacrifice the rigors of city life for the pleasures of the country and academia, an environment that I enjoyed years ago as a professor of economics.

Rather than let my credentials speak for themselves, I would enjoy meeting with you in person. Business frequently brings me to your area, so I will call you shortly to schedule an appointment.

With best regards,

LETTER 5-45   Telemarketing Sales

My first reaction was to call in response to your ad for a telemarketing rep so that you could experience my professional yet positive demeanor at once.

Instead, I am attaching my resume as your ad requested, providing you with in-depth information on the three years I have spent successfully resolving customer claims and accurately recording complex product orders with consistent praise from my supervisors.

Most important, I have enhanced my firm's reputation, keeping existing customers satisfied and transforming first-time buyers into loyal repeat purchasers.

I would welcome the chance to do the same for your organization and to speak with you directly.

Sincerely,

Here's an effective way to turn a negative into a positive. This jobhunter has held a string of jobs, but discusses this openly, presenting it as a benefit to the reader.

LETTER 5-46   Sales—Jobhopper—Job Loss

To the Yellow Pages Sales Manager:

Very few candidates possess a background such as mine—one that I'd like to put to work on your behalf.

As you'll see on my resume, the <u>depth of my experience</u> in sales offers you the opportunity to hire a genuine pro who needs little or no training and who is comfortable with and successful at cold calling.

Having worked as a Sales Rep in a variety of industries, I am skilled at developing sales pitches that are meaningful to the variety of businesses that advertise in the *Yellow Pages*... to turn interest into revenue for you. It is only due to the recent economic volatility (resulting in downsizing, layoffs, mergers, and business failures) that I have held positions at numerous companies. However, it is this fact that allows me to offer you such an unusual <u>breadth of experience</u>.

A personal interview would allow me to demonstrate my talents. I look forward to hearing from you so that we might schedule a meeting.

A focused, well-written letter such as this can put those of more experienced candidates to shame.

LETTER 5-47   Retail Sales—Workforce Return

In presenting myself as a candidate for the position of Sales Consultant at your bridal boutique, I present you with a valuable opportunity:

> **To hire an experienced expert who can simultaneously handle demanding, often stressed clientele with kid gloves.**

Having planned weddings for my own daughters, I am adept at dealing with the stress of the wedding gown selection and fitting process. Patiently, I assessed the virtues of lace, organza, tulle, and silk—the covered or off-the-shoulder design—knee, calf, or floor lengths. Gracefully, I balanced my daughters' concerns with those of their friends, husbands-to-be, and even mothers-in-law. Delicately, I increased our maximum budget as warranted to include all essential accessories. Conscientiously, I maintained our selection and fitting schedule. Unbelievably, I enjoyed it immensely—all three times!

Through it all, I was amazed to discover that my hands-on experience proved consistently more effective than that of our sales representatives, which is why I offer myself as a candidate.

After some time at home, I am now rejoining the workforce. I would welcome the opportunity to meet with you. If you will contact me via e-mail or phone (555-456-7890), I would be delighted to schedule an appointment to meet.

Sincerely,

LETTER 5-48   Retail Sales

I simply cannot resist responding to your job posting for a Sales Representative for your Windsor Mall Godiva Shop!

Solid sales experience is only the first of my qualifications—I have a successful track record and the recommendations to back it up.

Proven ability to translate consumer desires into purchase decisions is only the second of my qualifications—I have sold effectively within geographically and socioeconomically diverse markets.

Superior customer service delivery is only the third qualification I possess—I project warmth, enthusiasm, and a pleasant attitude.

Above all, and unlike almost everyone else in the world, I love chocolate but can resist the temptation to sample the inventory!

Combined, these qualifications make me an ideal candidate for your sales position. I hope you'll contact me for a personal interview.

Clever way to get attention.

LETTER 5-49 ▸ Senior Buyer—Confidentiality

If your job posting on CareerBuilder was written to attract my attention, it worked like a charm!

As the enclosed resume demonstrates, my background, experience, and proven accomplishments combine to make me the ideal Senior Buyer for Town and Country Home.

I have held a variety of positions in retail management with a particular emphasis in buying, having served as **a Buyer for Bloomingdale's with responsibility for both domestic and global purchasing**. In this position, I acquired a profound understanding of the unique preferences of the upscale consumer, which could help you avoid costly experiments with this demanding market segment.

My current involvement in the **development of innovative consumer product lines** will also be of value to you. I have been instrumental in engineering successful promotional programs that produced annual sales well over **$3 million** each.

Although I am secure in my current position, I realize that future growth may be limited. The opportunity to lend my expertise to Town and Country Home would be an exciting one. I hope you will give me a call so that we may schedule a convenient time to meet. Your discretion in contacting me is most appreciated.

LETTER 5-50   Director—Retail Operations

As Vice President of Retail Operations for a nationwide office supply chain, I reduced operating expenses by more than $2M last year. I further developed tightened security measures, accounting for a 50% reduction in losses due to employee and customer theft.

Proven results such as these are critical to your firm's profitability—and they are precisely what I can bring to Surplus Warehouse.

Having engineered the launch of 54 retail locations across the country, generating an additional $350M in sales, I am ideally equipped to direct your company in its ongoing expansion efforts.

These are only two chapters in a career story that spans 24 years in retailing. Additional successes, innovations, and cost-saving stories are detailed on the attached resume. Let's get together so that I can demonstrate the advantages that my experience can offer Surplus Warehouse.

LETTER 5-51 Distribution Manager—Salary

Over the years, I have been well aware of Inroads Automotive's continuing success.

As a customer and fellow member of the retailing profession, I have been impressed with the way your company stays ahead of your competition—by correctly predicting in advance what products and services the public will demand, and then delivering them.

This is exactly how I direct my professional career, which leads me to send you my resume now.

> **By carefully monitoring sales and industry trends, I significantly improved inventory management, increasing sales and broadening our customer base.**

> **I have also adapted MIS programs in conjunction with merchants to streamline inventory controls and reporting procedures without increasing expenses.**

In your search for a Distribution Manager, I hope you will consider me a serious candidate. When we meet, I will be pleased to provide information on my salary history as well as recommendations from previous employers.

I look forward to hearing from you.

LETTER 5-52   Senior Subcontracts Administrator—Confidentiality

RE: Monster.com posting for Senior Subcontracts Administrator

The position described in your post is the job I have been preparing for throughout my career.

- Having worked as both an assistant procurement manager and a subcontracts administrator for a major equipment manufacturer, I have mastered the tactics required to select, bid out, negotiate with, and manage independent vendors successfully.

- From my first day on the job, I will skillfully evaluate proposals, analyze risks, conduct contract negotiations, and perform cost analyses for you.

- I have handled in excess of 300 individual purchase orders simultaneously—some worth over $10M each.

- Most important, I have negotiated savings of up to 30% on new procurements.

As my resume attests, my experience is proven, and the results are measurable and substantial.

I would like to meet with you to further demonstrate my abilities. Please contact me via cell at (555) 765-4321 or e-mail at myname@ zmail.com, as my current employer is not aware of my desire to join another company.

LETTER 5-53   Accounts Receivable Coordinator—Salary

RE: TheLadders.com post for an Accounts Receivable Coordinator

Dear Mr. List:

Tact. Diplomacy. Presence. The traits that are most critical to success in collections are also the most difficult to find. I am pleased to offer you these indispensable skills—and more:

- Five years of experience in receivables billing, payment tracking, interest calculation, collection reporting, and customer database maintenance.

- Expertise in e-mail, live online chat, and telephone support.

- Solid third-party billing and collections experience.

- Mastery of QuickBooks, Sage, Capterra, and, of course, PayPal, Bill Pay, and PaySimple.

- Superior organizational and communication skills.

When we meet, you'll discover that, in hiring me, you immediately secure a professional who can work productively with your account executives to monitor past-due receivables and handle sensitive situations with firmness and delicacy—to support a productive team effort, not build an empire.

If you'll contact me at (555) 765-4321, we can schedule an interview to discuss my salary history in detail as well as this exciting opportunity.

LETTER 5-54 Financial Analyst—Recent MBA

RE: Your advertisement for a Financial Analyst

Are you searching for someone with a <u>thorough understanding</u> of the principles that support the operation of today's financial institutions and capital markets? Someone with the <u>ability</u> and <u>enthusiasm</u> to participate in investment decisions? Someone who is upbeat, is positive, learns quickly, and is <u>not afraid of hard work</u>?

If so, we should meet. As a graduate student at the University of Pennsylvania specializing in financial and international business, I expect to complete my MBA in May of this year. My goal is to put my <u>strong academic background in finance</u> to use in the world of business.

Throughout my graduate studies, I have focused on money and banking, international trade finance, and portfolio management. More specifically, I have conducted in-depth research on issues relating to:

- The functions of the central banks and their effects on the world economies.

- The operations of the world market and foreign exchange, as well as their impact on the U.S. economy.

- The underlying models of portfolio analysis, such as the capital asset pricing model and arbitrage pricing theory.

My resume, which is attached, further details my qualifications. I look forward to meeting with you to discuss how I can contribute to your company's bottom line.

I thank you in advance for your time and consideration.

LETTER 5-55   Financial Services—Student—Recent MBA

Ralph Enwood suggested that I contact you regarding the current opening in your brokerage division. With my MBA firmly in hand this coming May and several years of real-world experience, I would welcome the opportunity to contribute to the success your firm already enjoys.

I have attached my resume to supply specific information on my background. Allow me to provide you with the highlights:

- As a manager of finance for a discount brokerage group, I gained a profound understanding of the constant demands that a consumer customer base makes on traders and support staff—and how to meet these demands.

- I earned my Series 7 and Series 63 licenses while working full-time—a sound illustration of my work ethic and ability to complete simultaneous, challenging projects.

- I have been regularly praised by my superiors and professors for my written and verbal communication skills. I work well with others and enjoy assuming additional responsibility.

I would very much like to meet with you to explore your operations and the possibility of employment. The opportunity to join a winning team such as yours—and add to its success—is one I would relish.

LETTER 5-56   Cash Management Solutions Sales—Salary

RE: Monster.com posting for a Cash Management Solutions
Sales Officer

Six years of solid, in-depth banking experience. Expertise in handling
commercial relationships with businesses generating up to $50M in
sales. A commitment to new business development. This is what I can
bring to First Bancorporation, at once.

As an Assistant Vice President in Commercial Banking with BankUS,
I deal with a diverse client list—small to medium-sized companies, top executives of leading corporations, and accomplished (and
demanding!) celebrities. I am adept at identifying cash management
opportunities and providing solutions to short- and long-term cash-
flow needs for corporate clients.

As requested in your ad, I have uploaded my resume. My current
compensation includes base salary and commissions, and ranges from
$85,000 to $110,000 annually. I am anxious to set up a meeting with
you to discuss your position and my unique qualifications in greater
detail. I hope you will contact me at (555) 123-4567.

I look forward to speaking with you.

LETTER 5-57 **Private Banker**

States skills
gained—not
work history.

The attached resume details my achievements as an experienced private banker. However, it cannot demonstrate the maturity, insight, and new business development finesse I have acquired. These are the qualities I would like to show you firsthand.

Because I have worked closely with customers at every level—platform and private, retail and commercial—I have developed superior interpersonal skills, broad product knowledge, and a sure grasp of financial strategies and risk tolerance.

I can track down new business opportunities in an adverse economy. I can work effectively on my own while contributing fresh ideas to the team. I can learn from and support my coworkers with an attitude that is positive and pleasant.

May I demonstrate to you the advantages my experience can offer you? I will contact you again early next week to see when we might meet.

Sincerely,

LETTER 5-58   Lending Officer—Confidentiality

RE: Your job posting for a Lending Officer

Dear Mr. Harris:

I had the pleasure of speaking with you several years ago, and I thought I would write to you now in response to your recent post for a Lending Officer.

Since we last spoke, I have expanded my career in financial services and am now ideally qualified to excel as a superior Lending Officer. In addition to seven years of valuable banking experience, a BA in Economics, and an MBA, I can offer your clients vital capabilities, including, among others:

- Expertise in handling relationships of $50M or more.

- A history of achieving account profitability while ensuring client confidence and satisfaction.

- Mastery of analysis and recommendation for substantial commercial and personal loans.

I have attached an updated resume that details my training, professional experience, and accomplishments. If you would call, with discretion, (555) 456-7890, I would be happy to meet with you or anyone you might recommend.

I thank you in advance for any assistance you may provide.

LETTER 5-59 Senior Lender—Career Change

After working successfully for seven years as a consultant, I am now searching for a different challenge. Your organization came immediately to mind because of its reputation as a leading lender to entrepreneurial firms across the country.

The depth of experience I can offer would prove indispensable in your efforts to identify promising growth firms. I have worked with a broad range of companies, including: tech start-ups, mobile app developers, neutriceutical and pharmaceutical businesses.

My in-depth experience with entrepreneurs and companies with annual sales between $1M and $50M equips me to identify and assess the potential of growing firms with skilled management and promising sales. I have handled highly leveraged transactions, recapitalizations of LBO financings, turnarounds, workouts, and bridge financings.

Moreover, I have established long-term relationships with attorneys and accountants who have referred clients to me and will continue to do so.

I would welcome the opportunity to discuss with you the numerous benefits my background could provide to your firm. Let's get together to explore the possibilities. I will contact you to schedule an appointment.

| LETTER 5-60 | Research Director—Salary |

Dear Recruitment Director:

In your ad, you list five specific qualifications you seek in a research director to join your company. My background and experience enable me to meet each of your requirements, and then some.

For example, **you seek**...	and **I deliver**...
Fertilization production experience	years with Dow Chemical's soil enhancement division.
Management experience	Supervised a staff of 20 researchers in pursuit of water-soluble, environmentally safe microcatalyst.
Proven track record in research	Directed this team to identify successfully what is now the leading microcatalyst in use on American farms.
8 years' experience	10 years research, Dow Chemical; 4 years teaching, Cal Tech.
BSCE degree	BSCE degree, Johns Hopkins University

In addition, my teaching experience proved instrumental in presenting new technology to government officials in order to secure regulatory approval. I also served as liaison with the press to ensure correct introduction of the new product information.

As you can see, my strengths fit your requirements quite well. I would like to discuss my background with you in a personal meeting, at which time I would be happy to detail my salary history and expectations.

I can be reached at (555) 655-3210 during the daytime and (555) 345-4567 in the evening. I look forward to hearing from you.

International correspondence requires a more formal tone, which this writer has used.

LETTER 5-61   Environmental Engineering—International— Student—Language

I am writing to you at the recommendation of Madame Eugenie Enchant, Chief of the World Coalition Environment Program Regional Office, who suggested that my unusual qualifications might be valuable to WCEP's water-resource projects. I will be relocating to Beijing in May of 20XX to complete my Master's degree in Environmental Engineering, and I hope to join a project such as yours in September of that year.

My unique background, technical expertise, language abilities, and skill at coordinating multifaceted projects allow me to offer meaningful benefits to your project teams. After 13 years in the environmental field, as detailed on the attached resume, I have mastered the preparation of technical water-resource engineering analyses, community and regional planning reports, and comprehensive environmental impact studies. In addition, I can successfully manage complex engineering and planning projects and direct the positive, constructive interaction of the general public, clients, and government agencies.

I am comfortable in international settings, having spent a portion of my childhood in Europe and completed internships in Japan and Morocco; I am fluent in English, French, and Mandarin.

I would welcome the opportunity to explore how I might contribute to the World Coalition's Environment Program, particularly the WCEP water-resource protection and development programs in Africa, the Plan of Action for the Nogbutu River, and the desertification work for the Kalahari.

Thank you in advance for any insight you can offer.

LETTER 5-62 Security Officer

In a large corporation such as yours, the potential for employee misconduct is great. As you know, improprieties can have far-reaching consequences—for the company's performance, its credibility, and its other staff members.

> I can help you avoid such troubling circumstances through my ability to identify employee misconduct and then handle it according to proper legal procedures... yet with discretion.

My experience as a DEA Special Agent and Inspector General for the city's Housing Department is **unique among my peers**. These jobs have equipped me to **handle a variety of investigations,** including surveillance of employee time abuse, malfeasance, bribery, theft, improper reporting of sick leave, drinking violations, and others. My preparation for, and **participation in, hearings at the state and local level** will serve you well in those rare instances where litigation is necessary.

Hiring a proven professional like me can save you time, money, and all of the headaches associated with negative publicity. I will make myself available at your convenience for a personal meeting.

LETTER 5-63   Security Officer—Salary

With fewer resources upon which to draw, security officers working in the private sector frequently assume more varied and challenging responsibilities than many city police officers working as a team.

It's essential, therefore, that the private security officer you hire possesses in-depth experience, broad-based training, and the proven ability to perform in difficult, dangerous situations. A quick scan of this list of my abilities will prove that I am this officer:

- Undercover investigations

- Financial audits to identify drug-oriented profits; court-qualified expert in deciphering narcotics ledgers

- Coordination of complex interagency investigations

- Evidence handling and testimony

- Asset forfeiture investigations at state and federal level

- Adherence to policy and procedure

- National jurisdiction for drug-related offenses

- Licensed for weapons use

You'll find supplementary information on my resume, which is attached. I would like to prove my abilities to you further in a personal meeting, when we could discuss my salary history and requirements.

I hope to hear from you.

LETTER 5-64   Construction—Job Loss

After six years in construction, there is no doubt that this is where my skills and interest lie.

My resume (attached) describes the extensive range of projects on which I've worked, both commercial and residential. Throughout, I have received consistent praise from my superiors and have enjoyed the ongoing support of coworkers, many of whom have offered to serve as references for me.

The pressures of the current economic downturn have forced my employer to reduce his full-time staff. For this reason, I would welcome the opportunity to interview for a position at Felipe Construction. I hope you will contact me by e-mail or at (555) 456-7890.

LETTER 5-65   Building Superintendent—Job Loss—Language

Eleven years of hands-on experience as a building superintendent has made me more qualified than many others who may respond to your ad. The attached resume details my strengths; here is an overview:

- Experienced with both residential and commercial buildings
- Ability to supervise in-house maintenance staff and outside vendors, and to interact effectively with tenants
- Proficient in all aspects of maintenance, including plumbing and carpentry
- Valid #6 Oil, Standpipe, and Sprinkler System licenses
- Knowledgeable in tool inventory control and supply requisition
- Fluent in English and Spanish

As you can see, I possess solid, practical experience that I can put to use for you right away, as my present employer is relocating its headquarters out of state. If you will contact me via e-mail or phone (123-456-7890) I will be delighted to meet with you at your convenience. Thank you in advance.

This succinct summary worked well in response to an ad that was impossibly vague.

LETTER 5-66   Real Estate

I am writing to schedule a time for us to discuss the position mentioned in your ad. My background in real estate has equipped me with exceptional practical skills and an in-depth understanding of our industry. I would welcome the chance to explore how my strengths might contribute to the success of your firm.

Currently, I am involved in real estate as an owner, landlord, and building superintendent. As a result, I am completely familiar with legal regulations, housing requirements, construction, electrical, and plumbing. I am licensed in this state as a building inspector, EPA-Certified Radon Technician, and Pest Control Inspector. I am also working toward a Master's degree in Real Estate at State University. My qualifications are detailed in the attached resume.

I am eager to explore the possibility of working with your firm and would welcome the chance to meet in person.

LETTER 5-67   Real Estate Planner

In this challenging economy, organizations under pressure frequently relocate to reduce expenses. As a result, the relationship between real estate and overall strategic planning has become more crucial than ever.

Only a seasoned real estate professional like me can accurately balance the impact of real estate assets on your firm's business and financial strategy, profitability, and risk mitigation.

For more than 25 years, I have represented public- and private-sector clients in every aspect of the real estate transaction. I am now ready to offer my expertise to a company such as yours on a full-time basis.

Having worked in every type of major market, I can identify the properties that best meet your needs and negotiate optimal terms on your behalf. I have proven skill in dealing effectively with real estate experts, architects, space planners, construction estimators, financial analysts, and lawyers to streamline the planning process.

I hope you will contact me so that I can explain more in person about the advantages that my experience can deliver to your firm.

LETTER 5-68   Senior Architect—Relocation

I am responding to your ad for a Senior Architect for two reasons.

First, I can deliver precisely the attributes, experience, and background you seek in a senior architect. As you'll see on the enclosed resume, I have a strong background in commercial interiors and retail design, honed through 12 years with a major New York–based commercial firm.

In my current position, I assume all of the responsibilities typically demanded of a Senior Architect, including:

- Preparation of architectural plans, drawings, and specifications
- Construction and contract administration
- Review of design, code, and construction drawings
- Supervision of construction contractors and contract administration
- Project management through all project phases, including programming, planning, design, and construction contract administration

My conceptual abilities are outstanding, my approach is consistently team oriented, and I am an AutoCAD wizard! I earned my BA in Architectural Design from the State University Design School. These strengths, along with my clear knowledge of building architectural systems, construction procedures, and practices, will allow me to add value to your firm at once.

Second, I will be relocating to the Seattle area (and am in the process of obtaining Washington State licensure). It would be a privilege to meet with you personally to discuss the opportunity to add to your team.

LETTER 5-69   Social Media Manager

Your CareerBuilder post attracted my attention because I can offer you the precise qualifications you're seeking in a Social Media Manager—possibly at a lower cost than a more senior executive might demand, but with no less experience.

As you'll see on my resume, I currently serve as Associate Social Media Manager for OceanSail Clothing. Because the company's success depends upon its reputation in a specific market segment, I have worked strategically (and often around the clock) to ensure rapid responses to comments posted via social media. Of greater significance is that I successfully dispelled the false rumors about our company that followed the Bangladesh garment factory tragedy.

Expertise in social media is crucial to every successful business today; certainly my skill in deploying this talent to build user engagement and manage crises will prove immensely valuable to you. I would welcome the opportunity to meet with you.

LETTER 5-70 ▸ Director of Social Media

Social media is serious business. I urge you not to risk the trust that consumers have in your brand. It's strong, popular, and reputable. But that doesn't mean we can't grow it more, reach new markets, and expand its visibility and profitability. Bring me on your team and you secure a social expert with hard-to-match achievements, including:

- Development of highly successful $MM B2C social media strategies for the company brand, voice, and message, doubling monthly active Facebook users in 60 days.

- Redesign of social media branding strategy, execution launch, establishment of benchmarks in best practices, and implementation team leadership.

- Conception, creation, and management of user engagement programs across multiple social networks simultaneously that increased interaction on Facebook by 36% and on Twitter by 27%.

- Evaluation and implementation of cost-effective social monitoring and analytics.

You'll find more on my resume, along with specifics on my credentials, education, and certification. Many thanks,

LETTER 5-71	Content Manager

After six years as Senior Content Manager at the iconic start-up Artsy. com, I am eager to contribute my experience to a social enterprise of merit and meaning. In the Hope Water Foundation's effort to solve the world water crisis, you are working to create a brand, build awareness, and develop a global consumer base. In this work, I see a mission that I believe in and one that I can help succeed. Hope needs precisely what I did for Artsy:

- **Increased website traffic by 47%** in the first year by pioneering web marketing and social networking strategies, e-commerce innovations, and enterprise collaboration platforms.

- **Developed compelling content that engages prospects while meeting and exceeding SEO standards** via strategic deployment of trending, keyword, and buzz techniques and removing indexing barriers.

- **Drove revenue growth** by training and directing both staff and volunteers in strategy implementation to expand brand reach, engage users, promote useful content, and create an online presence for the organization and its brands.

Together, we can effect change quickly and effectively. Let's get started. The world needs us.

LETTER 5-72   Director of Telecommunications Technical Operations

In your search for an experienced, high-visibility leader to direct your Western Regional field operations, I present my credentials, which align ideally with those you are seeking. My resume details my experience and accomplishments, so I offer you several relevant highlights:

- Recognized leader with extensive experience running complete organizational structure, technical operations and all related financials, vendor and labor management, product marketing, offer management, and overall service delivery.

- Successfully hired, trained, developed, and directed sales and technical teams that deliver telecom, network, and IT services; have held full responsibility for contractual obligations, including engineering design and project delivery.

- Directed team of 90 elite Tier 3 Field Engineers, personally recruiting each member and growing overall team size by 200%. Handled all technical service field-related escalations around the world. Expanded technical proficiency of both service and client teams by pioneering the creation and implementation of performance labs.

- Directed 20+ elite service delivery teams in all aspects of complex telecommunications platform management for top 100 accounts, including Walmart, Burger King, Aetna, MetLife, HBO, U.S. Armed Forces, FBI, and DoD as well as state, county, and local municipalities.

- Generated $MM in new Fortune 1000 revenue through effective prospecting, development, RFP response and management, and executive briefings.

My career has paralleled the evolution of communications technology. I am gratified to have developed productive relationships with senior-level management and clients as well as strategic partnerships with organizations and providers of all types—all of whom cite my deep knowledge, insight, credibility, and integrity in representing the organization for which I work. I would welcome the chance to bring these vital advantages to yours.

LETTER 5-73   Recruiter

When you hire a recruiter with more than 10 years of experience in the financial services industry, you can be certain that you've hired someone who knows who, what, when, how, and for how much to hire the staff members you need to grow.

My 10 years of experience in both corporate and field sales environments have equipped me to manage the entire hiring process, from sourcing to decision making, including:

- Developing a sourcing strategy that employs online job postings, employee referral programs, centers of influence, job fairs, and open houses.

- Conducting all initial interviews; scheduling, coordinating, and evaluating all successive interviews with key managers.

- Screening, testing, and evaluating candidates.

- Consulting with managers, effecting and implementing final hiring decisions.

You'll find all the details on the attached resume. You'll find me ready, willing, and able to meet with you at your convenience.

LETTER 5-74 **E-learning Director**

My skills and experience are an ideal fit for your position of E-learning Director with social media expertise. During my four years with the Waters boutique hotels, I managed the Online Learning Center, the corporate website, and the creation and placement of branded social content. My achievements include:

- Led the development and implementation of appropriate Online Learning Center content; ensured strategic alignment with website.

- Personally secured meaningful, relevant content by cultivating strategic partnerships with recognized SMEs, internal and external content developers.

- Generated additional revenue by developing opportunities for monetizing Learning Center content.

- Increased engagement, supported and promoted the corporate sales team's business development efforts by facilitating a constant flow of information and education.

These achievements, and others detailed on my resume, illustrate what I can do for your organization. I would welcome the opportunity to discuss, in person or via Skype, the benefits I can offer. Thank you for your consideration.

LETTER 5-75 E-learning Manager

Subject: Being a Superior Global E-learning Manager

Being an E-learning Manager involves more than planning, implementing, and managing online courseware... and more than developing new e-learning products, services, and systems—all of which I can handle better than anyone.

Being a superior E-learning Manager means serving as the champion of e-learning within your organization so that your staff buys into this technology. The difference lies in experience and attitude—both of which I would be delighted to deliver. For example, I can:

- Develop strategic e-learning plans for each business unit.

- Seamlessly supervise remotely located staff.

- Nurture strong relationships with internal clients so that change becomes palatable, even welcome.

- Communicate effectively throughout all levels of the organization.

- Thrive in a fast-paced, ever-changing, multitasking environment.

- Partner with classroom training to design blended learning paths.

- Work with expense controls and within budgetary parameters.

I am as committed to e-learning as I will be to your firm. I hope you'll allow us to discuss this exciting opportunity. As soon as I hear from you, I will adjust my schedule so that we can meet.

LETTER 5-76   Internet Sales Representative—Salary

As at many firms, my company's recent downsizing left too many tasks to too few people. Therefore, my three years at CompNet were packed with opportunities that are not usually available to a recent college graduate. As a result, I am younger than many people with my depth of experience—which means I can offer you talent and energy at a lower price!

Thanks to the explosion of online sales, I gained a profound understanding of the who, when, what, how, and why of Internet selling, and which segments of this highly profitable market respond to which products, offers, and price points. This is valuable knowledge that I can bring to your organization from day one to enhance your marketing efforts and help achieve your sales goals.

My current salary is $60K plus benefits. I would like to bring my skills to a firm that is able to offer a salary in the $75–100K range. I would welcome the chance to meet with you and will adjust my schedule so that we can do so right away.

This unique opening not only gets attention, but it also builds credibility. Notice that the writer refers to the attached descriptions of her experience and skills, but uses this e-mailed cover letter to focus on how effectively she uses them on her employer's behalf. Very effective!

LETTER 5-77   Information Architect

For the opening you advertised online, please allow my colleague to introduce me:

"Sophia is an outstanding professional with proven talent in designing solutions that not only ideally address our clients' concerns, but also anticipate them. She flawlessly directs the implementation of new processes and programs as she gracefully manages multifaceted, global information operations. She is a pleasure to work with as both a team member and a leader."—William Bennes (555-123-4567)

To substantiate Bill's generous remarks, I have attached to this note:

- My resume detailing my substantial experience with Fortune 500 corporations and their clients.

- A listing of the numerous technologies, operating systems, applications, and software I have mastered.

- Highlights of the numerous successful projects I have spear-headed, many of which produced profits or savings of hundreds of thousands of dollars for my firm's clients.

As I hope you'll agree, my qualifications are both sound and profound—as are the contributions they will enable me to make for your organization and its clients. I would welcome the opportunity to present these qualifications in person. Please contact me at any of the phone numbers provided below, or via e-mail.

Thank you for your consideration.

LETTER 5-78   Java Programmer—Salary—Relocation

Subject: Exceptional Java Programmer

The exceptional Java Programmer must display specific technical proficiency, as I do:

As you'll see on the attached resume, I possess absolute mastery of Core Java, including memory leak, memory management, garbage collection, data structures, and threads in Java, as well as developing Java web applications with JEE technologies: JSP, Servlets, JNDI, JDBC, and JMS. I am familiar with OOP and adept at using relational databases (Oracle x or SQL Server) and at designing and setting up relational databases, manipulating relational data, file structures, and creating data models.

But the exceptional Java Programmer must also possess qualities that will contribute to the overall success of the team, the division, the corporation, and its clients, as I do:

- Exemplary experience designing fully integrated, highly scalable, cost-effective, end-to-end solutions that meet or beat industry best practices.
- Formidable communication skills that equip me to describe complex architecture and technologies to IT business units, clients, and colleagues at every level.
- Proven success in project presentation, technical documentation, and serving as a technical contributor to a multideveloper project team.

In response to your query, I am currently earning the equivalent of $85,000 annually, including base salary, benefits, car, expense account, bonus, and incentives. However, as I am anxious to work with a firm of your stature, and to relocate to the West Coast, I can be flexible on initial salary level, assuming there is room for growth. I will be in your area for the next month and would be thrilled to meet for an interview. Please contact me via e-mail or cell phone.

Thank you in advance for your consideration,

LETTER 5-79   Network Administrator

What a thrill it would be to bring my experience, knowledge, and energy to your firm. I have attached my resume; you'll see that I possess all of the qualifications you seek.

I have a combined background in system and network administration, including installation and configuration of routers, switches, servers, and desktops. What's more, I am experienced with:

- Exchange Server 2007/2010
- Small Business Server
- Terminal Server and remote desktop/remote access
- VoIP phone installation
- PC break/fix and tier 1 and 2 ticket resolution of hardware andsoftware

As a result, you can count on my expertise for seamless handling of server upgrades, migrations, implementations, and updates as well as configuring switches, VLANs, firewalls, and routers. I can resolve complex technical hardware and software problems while managing and maintaining the complete IT infrastructure environment to support the operations and continued success of your business.

Should we have the opportunity to meet, you'll discover what my resume cannot reveal—that I am a professional who can work both independently and in a team environment. That I interact effectively with disparate business units, project management, and quality control teams. That I enjoy mentoring fellow team members. That I excel in an environment that is replete with rapid change, frequent challenges, and mind-boggling deadlines . . .

. . . and that I would be thrilled to be part of your IT team.

LETTER 5-80   Systems Software Development Manager—Veteran

The systems development background I've detailed on the attached resume has equipped me with a deep knowledge of tightly integrated digital technologies and wireless connectivity.

Both in the corporate arena and during two tours of duty in Afghanistan, I acquired in-depth experience in building and leading teams of engineers in the design, development, test, and deployment of a range of products on a range of platforms.

Using my technical, project management, and communication skills, I directed these talented specialists in developing production-quality code that proved reliable, maintainable, and scalable and that fulfilled business objectives while ensuring innovative end-user-facing website solutions.

You'll find me a valuable addition to your management team. I possess a master's degree in Computer Science; experience porting firmware to new hardware platforms and integrating new hardware capabilities; mastery of Java, C/C++, Objective-C, Python, and open-source technologies (Linux, SQLite, OpenGL, BusyBox); and development experience on mobile platforms such as Google Android, WebOS, Windows Mobile, Apple iPhone, and RIM BlackBerry.

It would be a genuine opportunity to apply my unusual capabilities to help your firm land and support lucrative contracts, enhancing your overall reputation and success. Thank you for your interest.

LETTER 5-81   MIS Manager—Salary

As an experienced and successful MIS Manager, I offer all of the qualifications listed in your job posting—and then some. I am, therefore, submitting my resume, which illustrates that I have the experience, technical proficiency, and expertise to do all of the following effectively:

- Plan, coordinate, direct, and design all internal IT-related activities to streamline operations, increase staff productivity, and enhance revenue growth.

- Develop and implement IT policies and procedures, including those for architecture, security, disaster recovery, purchasing, and service provision.

- Coordinate upgrades on hardware, software, and remote access technologies; install new system software releases; execute preventative maintenance and repair; and manage equipment inventory and maintenance.

- Create and maintain the operations and procedures manual, and review system and operations documentation to assure compliance with organizational benchmarks and industry best practices.

I look forward to being productive for you right from the start—with little to no training—as my expertise is broad: LAN administration, UNIX, NT, Windows 9x, Microsoft Office, Norton Ghost, Active Directory, GPOs and DNS, DHCP, MS Exchange, and IEEE-based networking fundamentals.

The benefit of my current position at a start-up is that I had the opportunity to handle a range of responsibilities. The downside is that my salary history may not be aligned with industry standards. I would be pleased to provide you with more information on this when we have the chance to meet. If you will contact me at (555) 765-4321, I will be pleased to set up an appointment.

This unusually bold approach works because the candidate meets every one of the requirements listed in the ad.

LETTER 5-82   Network Administrator—Confidentiality

Your advertisement addresses my qualifications so ideally, one would think we'd met. And we should—because I can offer you the precise skills for which you're searching.

You seek the ability to:	Do I possess?
Identify network requirements; install upgrades; monitor network performance; manage data backups and disaster recovery operations.	YES
Lead team in deploying technologies such as SAN, VLAN, wired and wireless LAN and WAN switching and routers for voice, data, and video.	YES
Maintain user accounts, profiles, file sharing, access privileges, and security; perform daily server tape backups.	YES and YES
Manage IT team to ensure 24/7 support and handle Help Desk calls.	YES

I hope you'll agree that your needs and my capabilities are a perfect match, because it would be a thrill to join a firm with the technological talent that yours employs.

Attention grabber.

In fact, I am not currently in the job market, but am responding <u>only to your ad</u>. Therefore, I would appreciate maintaining confidentiality. Please contact me at home at (555) 456-7890 evenings or weekends, or by e-mail. I'd be pleased to set up a meeting whenever it's convenient for you.

Sincerely,

LETTER 5-83 Mobile and Web Applications Developer— Part-Time/Full-Time

Designing intuitive, innovative mobile web applications is a creative endeavor that requires in-depth knowledge, hands-on experience, and the ability to think logically, strategically, and out-of-the-box all at the same time. It's a tall order. But it's one I can fill for you; as you'll see on the attached resume, I can deliver:

- Six years of full-cycle application architecture development experience, including successful interactions with UX/UI, product management, and other teams.
- Mastery of Android and iOS operating systems as well as web UI technologies, including HTML5, CSS, and JavaScript.
- High-level proficiency in C, C#, C++, ASP.net, HTML, jQuery Mobile, Xcode, Visual Studio, and MySQL.
- Productive collaboration with systems engineers and quality assurance teams to troubleshoot releases.

Moreover, I am passionate about partnering with business development, branding, and design teams to shape world-class products that ensure a delightful and engaging experience to users around the world.

I hope you will consider me a serious candidate for the opening; I am pleased to work on a full-time salaried or contract basis.

LETTER 5-84   Client/Server Architect

More than technical proficiency, my in-depth experience as a systems developer has equipped me to deliver expert judgment and analysis in the design, development, and implementation of client/server systems.

In addition to value-adding capabilities in software and agile systems development, I have worked with Linux, Perl, Oracle, ColdFusion, WebSphere AS, and WebSphere MQ core platforms and development tools.

As a result, I offer you essential advantages that others may not, including the ability to immediately:

- Drive teams in successful systems development, architectural design, integration of web applications, and data systems.

- Apply technical insight to the evaluation, implementation, optimization, operation, and maintenance of web-based reporting and business intelligence systems.

- Collaborate effectively with other systems development and IT maintenance organizations in defining system requirements, recommending and implementing performance enhancements that meet operational and budgetary requirements.

As both a technology and a team leader, my expertise and record of achievement are at your disposal. It would be an honor to join an organization with your reputation for integrity and innovation. Please feel free to contact me at any time at (555) 456-7890 or by e-mail at PatScillo@zmail.com.

Without providing more detail than is necessary, this jobhunter arms the recruiter with valuable information: his field, his specialty, and what he offers an employer.

LETTER 5-85 Electrical Engineer—Job Loss

In today's difficult economy, you undoubtedly receive hundreds of resumes from people seeking employment. However, you have built a career on the ability to recognize marketable talents, which I possess—in-depth experience, focused expertise, flexibility, adaptability, commitment, and a highly effective management style.

My current employer's economic health makes it advisable for me to seek a new situation as soon as possible. I am therefore taking the liberty of forwarding my resume for your review.

My specific niche is the design and implementation of new technology for electrical subsystems, but I can contribute effectively within a variety of engineering environments.

My background, professional experience, and work style equip me to offer a rare overview of the field along with a profound grasp of project details. This mix is unusual among professionals in my field, and it is essential to the employer who is actively seeking innovative solutions in emerging technologies.

I look to your expertise for assistance in my search and will call you early next week to see whether we can schedule a meeting. I thank you in advance for your consideration.

Excellent opening for recruiter letter.

LETTER 5-86   CRM Director

To devise strategies that drive acquisition, customer retention, loyalty, and revenue growth requires deep CRM knowledge and experience. I am pleased to present my qualifications, which I am confident fulfill your requirements ideally.

Deep CRM Knowledge and Experience. My 10-year career has afforded me the chance to work in all aspects of customer relationship management, from segmentation and lead acquisition/nurturing/conversion to marketing planning and implementation.

Demonstrated CRM Success. I have directed innovative and highly effective retention/loyalty initiatives using digital and online channels, including search, display, affiliate, social, and mobile, that significantly increased sales while strengthening market position and brand equity.

Advanced Skills. You'll benefit immediately from my exceptional analytical skills and ability to collaborate with IT partners to develop processes and infrastructure to support scalable loyalty and CRM programs and with cross-functional teams in order to explore and build new revenue streams.

Value-Adding Strengths. Recognized for best practice insight, for understanding of back-end technologies and reporting architectures, and for fostering enterprisewide endorsement of CRM culture.

If you're seeking a successful, influential, and passionate CRM leader, let's schedule a time to meet without delay. I am eager to explore the possibility of joining your impressive organization.

To see the results this heartfelt letter produced, see the follow-up in Letter 6-14.

LETTER 5-87   Teaching Artist

RE: Your ad for a Teaching Artist, *Community Times*, 4/10/XX

What a delight it is to discover a school that recognizes the value of promoting dance among its students and actually allocates funding for this vital intention!

In applying for the teaching position at the Lincoln Center Institute, I offer you a rare mix of talents and experience, as described in detail on the attached resume. My **comprehensive training** in the United States and abroad is complemented by my experience as a **member of such diverse companies** as the Belgrade National Theatre, the Ballet Hispanico of New York, and the Juilliard Dance Ensemble. This training and experience have equipped me to introduce to students a far broader range of methods, techniques, styles, music, and interpretation than many others in the field.

Throughout more than 20 years in dance and dance education, I have experienced my own joy as well as that of students of every age and skill level as they acquire much-needed self-confidence by expressing themselves through movement. The opportunity to continue such a worthwhile endeavor at the Lincoln Center Institute would be as thrilling as it would be rewarding.

I will contact you within the next several days to further explore this exciting possibility.

Thank you for your consideration.

LETTER 5-88   Teacher—Career Change

As a father with three children in the Milford school system, I hope that each of my children not only receives a sound education, but also acquires a perspective on life outside the school walls. With my business background and teaching credentials, I am equipped to offer both to the Milford students.

After 20 years in corporate business training, I am now shifting my focus to educating within the school system. This year, I completed my education credits, fulfilled my student teaching requirements at Milford Middle School, and passed my certification exams. Having just received word from Albany that my Certificate of Qualifications has been issued, I thought this would be the ideal time to write to you.

My diverse background offers Milford students a unique opportunity to discover how their studies have practical application in what they call "the real world."

I would welcome the chance to discuss any openings that may arise under your aegis. I will contact you soon to see whether we might meet, or you may reach me at (555) 765-4321.

Most sincerely,

Here is a novel approach that works for a graduating student with no relevant background.

LETTER 5-89   Kindergarten Teacher—Student—Career Change

With great excitement, I am responding to your ad for a Kindergarten Teacher. The opportunity to teach in the school system that fostered my interest in education is a thrilling one.

Because I have recently switched from the business world to teaching, my resume may not provide the information you require (it is attached, nonetheless). Instead, allow me to excerpt from a recommendation provided by my advisor, Lynn Karyli:

> "Lauren never seems to choose the easy way; she takes the most demanding courses, opts to work in the most challenging teaching situations, attempts the most innovative and difficult teaching approaches, and volunteers time and energy to extracurricular activities. And, in all her endeavors, she is successful....

> "It should be noted that in the short period of a year and a half, Lauren won the praise and admiration of her professors and her peers. She was selected as research assistant for a project on children's response to the arts. She is a highly respected member of her peer group, valued both for her leadership capabilities and for her constructive feedback and support of the efforts of others....

> "Thus, Lauren is a model for all who are associated with her, and to all she brings enthusiasm and energy, sensitivity, thoughtfulness, and thoroughness, and above all, a love of children and of life."

This recommendation (in its entirety) is also attached. I am anxious to pursue this opportunity and to meet you in person. I will take the liberty of calling you to schedule an appointment.

Sincerely,

LETTER 5-90   Teacher—Part-Time/Full-Time—Relocation

As a teacher of English at the Forsyth Satellite Academy in New York City, I will soon complete the Master's Program in English Education at New York University, where I have the honor of having been selected as the Graduate Valedictory Speaker. This summer, I will receive six postgraduate credits as a participant in the New York City Writing Project at the City University of New York. Before entering the field of education, I enjoyed eight years in accounting—a field I left voluntarily in January of 20XX to pursue a long-felt desire to teach, motivate, and guide students in their use of the language and appreciation of literature. I am thrilled with my decision to switch careers!

With these unique strengths, I write because I am moving to Cape Cod in August, and I seek a position as a teacher of English in the Provincetown School District.

I recognize that there may be a shortage of openings. While my primary goal is to secure a full-time position teaching English, I would like to offer my services in any capacity for which you might find my background suitable. I will gladly work on a part-time basis or as a substitute. I have attached a resume of my business and educational experience along with my most recent evaluation, made by my practicum supervisor.

I would welcome the privilege of meeting with you to discuss any appropriate position that you may have in your district. I can come to see you on very short notice should you be willing to meet with me; you can reach me at (555) 235-3456. Thank you for your consideration.

The lack of a resume is not holding back this homemaker and mother from applying for a job. Her letter sounds and looks as professional as that of any executive.

LETTER 5-91 Child-Care Worker—Workforce Return

Seton Day Care, its children, and their parents deserve the very best child-care worker you can find. May I offer myself as a candidate who can meet this tough standard?

<u>My experience working with children is as extensive as it is diverse</u>. As a mother of two, I have performed the numerous and continual duties that caring for every newborn demands. As a volunteer in both the nursery school and first-grade classroom environments, I have dealt effectively with children at an age when your every breath and action contributes to the shaping of their personalities, demeanor, and morals. I have also cared for older children in my home, both for pay and as a courtesy to other mothers, so I am well aware of the challenges and rewards of this vital responsibility.

<u>Supporting my practical experience is a thorough educational background and hands-on work in the field</u>. In earning my degree in Family and Consumer Studies, my relevant studies included courses in Child Psychology, Child Development, Sociology of the Family, and Family Relationships. In addition, I completed fieldwork in an urban day care facility.

<u>Personally, I offer you the following strengths</u>: I possess a calm attitude and a superb understanding of children's needs. Many people are surprised by how comfortable their children feel with me. As a mother, I empathize with other parents and find it easy to build a productive rapport.

Although I am in the process of updating my resume, I am extremely interested in pursuing this opportunity, and I did not want to delay contacting you. At your convenience, I would like to meet with you to explore the opportunity of working together. If you will contact me at (555) 456-7890 (day or evening), we can schedule a meeting, at which I will present you with my completed resume.

Thank you in advance for your consideration.

LETTER 5-92   Social Worker—Geriatric

I am writing to explore the exciting possibility of joining your team at Winterhaven, building on my success as a social worker in the respiratory and medical intensive care units at Saint Helen's Medical Center.

With master's degrees in both ethics and social work, I am particularly interested in end-of-life issues that surface within the geriatric population and, in particular, the role of social workers in developing and supporting a sense of pride and place in the lives of the elderly.

While in my social work internship during graduate school, I sought to develop this sense of pride by helping my patients create ethical wills, in which they articulated, proudly and with purpose, the accomplishments they had made throughout their lifetimes and the values they held dear and now wanted to pass on to future generations. I hope to continue fostering this kind of purpose in the lives of the elderly— whether through ethical wills, psychosocial counseling, bereavement support, or other vehicles of service—as a member of your social work team.

Please find attached my resume for your review. I would very much appreciate having the opportunity to speak in person and will make myself available at your convenience.

If you were hiring, it's likely that you'd find it tough to turn down an interview with someone so skilled and dedicated. Despite being out of the workforce for years, this jobhunter knows how to get results!

LETTER 5-93   Social Worker—Workforce Return

Dear Mr. Girannelli:

Your ad for a social worker caught my attention, since I would like to rejoin the profession after several years as a homemaker and mother. With my education, experience, and commitment to human services, I possess all the qualifications you seek.

I have a BS in Learning Disabilities, an MSW degree, and a state social work license. For five years, I worked at a facility providing subacute care and rehabilitation services to children with a variety of special health needs and their families, receiving regular praise from my superiors for my clinical and interpersonal skills. More recently, I performed more than 10,000 hours of volunteer work with substance abusers while raising three children.

Through my efforts over the years, I have remained abreast of new issues and ideas in human services. I would be surprised if you were able to find a more dedicated employee than I will be, or one who is more ready to contribute once again by performing first-class assessments, treatments, consultation, and training.

Attached you will find my resume, a copy of my state license, and a list of references. If there is anything else I can provide, please let me know. I am anxious to meet with you.

LETTER 5-94   Speech Pathologist—Student

If your Speech Pathology Department has room for a skilled, enthusiastic, and committed speech therapist, I hope you will consider me.

This June, I will receive my BS from State University's School of Speech. I have already begun supplementing my formal training in speech and language pathology with several practicums and internships, all of which inspire me to continue contributing to this valuable profession while preparing for my master's and certification.

Through my work with stroke patients, stutterers, and those with cleft palate and articulation disorders, I have acquired hands-on experience that may enhance the success and reputation that your department already enjoys. My grades and evaluations have been consistently superior, validating my skill as well as my ability to work harmoniously with coworkers.

Of greatest value to you, however, is my commitment to each and every patient with whom I work. My objective is to improve their lives by improving their abilities to communicate and their self-esteem.

If these are the qualities you seek, I hope you will contact me. I will be happy to visit your office for an interview, at your convenience.

LETTER 5-95   Registered Nurse—Workforce Return

RE: Your msnhealth.com posting for a Registered Nurse

Given the reputation for excellence that you maintain at the Sacred Heart Academy, you hold equally rigorous standards in your search for a Registered Nurse to care for your students and faculty.

Excellence is exactly what I can deliver, along with an unusually strong background in healthcare.

My resume, which is attached, details the depth of my experience with newborns, grade-level children, adolescents, and young adults. As you'll see, I have worked as a Student Health Nurse, Camp Nurse, Family Camp Coordinator, hospital Staff Nurse in labor and delivery, and Nursing Care Coordinator. These assignments, along with my work as a Nurse Coordinator for a Perinatal HIV Transmission study, honed my ability to deal with children and their parents with understanding, warmth, and humor.

During the past several years, I reduced my workload outside the home while raising two sons. I am now ready and eager to return to nursing, and to continue combining exceptional medical care with compassionate patient care.

The opportunity to pursue these objectives as a member of Sacred Heart's highly respected staff is an important one. I do hope that you'll allow me to present my qualifications to you in person.

LETTER 5-96 Registered Nurse/Quality Improvement
Program Director

To the Director of Human Resources for St. Andrew's Hospital:

I am responding to your ad for a Registered Nurse to direct your
Quality Improvement Program because I can supply *precisely* the background you require.

My resume supports the following introduction:

- I earned my MS in nursing at State College.

- I have worked for three years as Assistant Director of
  Quality Assurance under Janice Powers at State Hospital.

- I am adept at interpreting quality assurance standards to
  ensure adherence to DPH and JCAHO guidelines.

- I have assisted in the creation of quality improvement
  policies, compiling statistical data and writing narrative
  reports that summarize quality assurance findings.

- I have directed a variety of health center personnel and
  worked with numerous patients in order to evaluate the
  effectiveness of this quality improvement program.

Of greatest importance is my commitment to ensuring comprehensive, easily accessible, high-quality care. My in-depth experience has
prepared me to define and implement quality improvement standards
that function in full compliance with existing health center policies
and procedures.

I am fully prepared to assume complete responsibility for directing a
Quality Improvement Program, and I would welcome the opportunity
to explore how my skills meet your specific needs.

This jobhunter has categorized his abilities so that the letter can be easily skimmed—or read in full with greater meaning. Either way, any reader will be convinced that he is a qualified candidate worth interviewing.

LETTER 5-97 Senior Pharmacist—Job Loss

RE: Your Glassdoor.com listing for a Senior Pharmacist

My qualifications are ideal for the position you've advertised—and since my current employer has been acquired by a major retailer, I am available to you almost immediately. My resume, which is attached, details my training, licensure, and professional experience. Allow me to highlight my strengths and capabilities for you here:

Competency. Experience. I routinely and accurately ensure proper filling and dispensing of prescriptions; evaluate physician drug orders and patient profiles for appropriateness of therapy, dose, and dosing regimens; and clarify and correct problematic drug orders.

Interaction with Physicians and Patients. I effectively obtain patient medical and medication histories; answer inquiries from physicians and patients regarding drug therapies, drug dosing and administration, drug interactions, adverse effects, and new products; provide direct patient counseling and education; advise patients on prescription-related insurance benefits; monitor patient profiles for drug interactions and allergies; and provide courteous customer service and professional relations.

Accurate Recordkeeping. I ensure proper documentation of pharmacy records in accordance with state law and handle prescription inventory control and management.

Insurance and Claims Expertise. I operate automatic claims verification programs and assure proper billing to third-party insurance providers; correspond with insurance providers regarding patient eligibility and benefits; and maintain accounts receivable records for third-party payers.

Inventory Control. I correspond with wholesalers to determine the availability and cost of drug products; track cost of goods sold, sales, gross margin percent, accounts payable, and inventory turns on a weekly basis; and maintain records of prescription sales and volume, and compare these to previous periods in order to improve inventory management.

I am available to meet as early as next week, if that meets your timing requirements. Thank you in advance for your consideration.

LETTER 5-98   Assistant Director, Emergency Medical Services—
Salary—Language

To Los Angeles County Officials:

I am eager to present myself as a candidate for the Assistant Director of Emergency Medical Services for Los Angeles County. It has long been a dream of mine to contribute to the safety of residents and public protection professionals at the county level.

I am proud to report that, in addition to meeting all of the qualifications listed in your advertisement—and being fully bilingual in Spanish and English—I also offer you the following important strengths:

Diverse Supplemental Training. I have complemented my education and training, successfully completing additional courses in critical incident stress response, aircraft emergency incident management, emergency response to hazardous materials incidents, prehospital response to radiation accidents, emergency vehicle operation, poison control, and crash victim extrication.

Proven Ability to Perform. During my 12-year career with the Oakland Township Emergency Medical Service, I served as EVOC Instructor before being promoted from Paramedic to Lieutenant of Special Operations to Captain of the Training Division. Currently, I serve as the EMS Liaison to the township's Medical Advisory Committee.

Solid Teaching Background. At Oakland Memorial Hospital's Institute of Emergency Medicine, I served as an instructor for the Paramedic Training Program, EMT, and CPR training. I also directed the Oakland Police Department's Vehicle Extrication program.

Recognized for Excellence. Throughout my career, I have received praise for my contributions, including more than 50 letters of commendation, 20XX and 20XX Township Life Saving Medals, and the Fire Department's Award of Merit, among other distinctions.

Since your position offers an opportunity, location, and benefits package that are very appealing to me, my salary requirements are flexible. I would be honored if you would consider me a serious candidate.

LETTER 5-99 Personal Trainer—Job Loss

RE: Monster.com ad for a Personal Trainer

In our industry, turnover is high among training staff, and this often adversely affects customers' perceptions of a health club or fitness center. I can help your organization avoid this problem.

I have been in my current position for nine years, and am seeking alternative employment because our owner has decided to retire and close the facility. Not only do I have the experience to bring to your club, but I have also built a loyal base of "one-on-ones," many of whom are likely to follow me within reasonable geographic limits.

I am well versed in a complete range of equipment, such as aerobic (StairMaster, treadmills, running machines, cross-country skiing, bicycles, Lifecycle, and VersaClimber), free weights, Universal, Eagle, and Nautilus. I have designed personal fitness programs for clients from ages 18 to 80, even working successfully with individuals required by their doctors to lose 100 pounds or more. My skill, rapport, and results have led many of my existing clients to introduce me to their friends, whom I have brought into the facility as new clients.

If you're looking to add long-lasting muscle to your training program, please contact me at (555) 456-7890, and we can schedule a time to get together.

LETTER 5-100   Esthetician

RE: Indeed.com post for an Esthetician

When working with clients, my goals are to pamper the mind and body... soothe muscle tension... relieve stress... eliminate fatigue due to overwork. . .

. . . The very same benefits you'll enjoy when you add a professional, experienced esthetician to your staff. And few are as accomplished as I am.

Naturally, I am skilled at blending concentrated therapeutic oils for aromatherapy massage to create the optimal ambience for effective beauty treatments. But I am also well versed in a complete range of revitalizing regimens, including facial and body skin care, body scrub and polishing, tissue toning, hydrotherapy, seaweed body mask, and detoxification.

The result is that by hiring me, you acquire a range of additional services to offer your clients for the price of a single expert esthetician. Plus, I can bring with me an established, affluent base of regular clientele.

I firmly believe in the importance of massage and esthetic treatments to combat stress and prevent illness, and would appreciate the opportunity to demonstrate my abilities firsthand.

If you would be kind enough to contact me at my home number, I will be pleased to schedule an appointment to discuss how my varied skills can relieve the pressure for you and your staff.

LETTER 5-101 Dental Hygienist—Part-Time/
Full-Time—Confidentiality

After 12 years as a dental hygienist, I know all there is to know about routine oral hygiene, orthodontic hygiene, and pediatric hygiene.

However, my experience extends further than this... and further than that of other hygienists.

I have performed in a frenetically busy multipractitioner environment as well as in a teaching facility. As a result, I am expertly capable of managing the demands of overworked dentists, nervous adults, and hyperactive children. I can instantly develop a comforting rapport with patients of any age.

Now, I would like to apply my expertise to the needs of a small, local practice. From the sound of your HealthCallings.com job posting, my skills would be a perfect match for your setting. Although I am looking for a full-time position, I would willingly accept the challenge described in your ad: that successful performance could lead to regular part-time or full-time employment.

If you will contact me at either my home or cell phone number, I will be delighted to set up a meeting at your convenience. I would greatly appreciate your understanding in refraining from contacting my present employer at the moment.

Thank you for your consideration.

LETTER 5-102   Chauffeur—Job Loss

RE: Craigslist ad for a Chauffeur

STOP! Don't read another resume—except mine. My five years' experience as a chauffeur for the CEO of a Fortune 500 company equips me with the precise qualifications you seek.

MERGE my professional appearance and demeanor with the ability to perform around the clock, discretion, and the utmost caution—and you secure the most reliable, personable chauffeur available.

TURN your attention to the telephone and call me at (555) 765-4321, and I will come in at once for an interview. My current employer has retired to the Caribbean, so I am available to begin working immediately.

I thank you in advance for your consideration.

Here's a jobhunter who knows her industry! The opening, body, and close are consistent with her knowledge and tone of voice.

LETTER 5-103   Editorial Assistant

RE: Your posting for an Editorial Assistant

The value of your delightful AspenGlow mysteries, which I avidly consumed as a child, remains unmatched in my life.

From this series, I acquired the ability to persevere in the search for a more effective method... skepticism when faced with a too-obvious solution... the curiosity to discover what more a person can offer. Each of these traits was inspired by AspenGlow. All are qualifications that the successful editor must possess.

The older I get, the more I appreciate what Frick Publishing and AspenGlow brought to my life. And as I am still far from retirement, I am able to bring these talents back to you. I have attached my resume to demonstrate that my experience is as relevant as my enthusiasm.

I would appreciate the opportunity to meet in person so that you may consider me as a serious candidate for the position of editorial assistant.

LETTER 5-104 ▸ Employee Benefits Manager

RE: Monster.com ad for an Employee Benefits Manager

Employee benefits are as vital to your organization as they are to your staff. However, the details inherent in most benefits plans can make administering them cumbersome and time-consuming—which is why you are now seeking an experienced professional. In me, you have found one.

As you'll see on the attached resume, I have managed all aspects of a comprehensive benefits program, including complex healthcare programs, COBRA, and the new Affordable Care Act regulations. Of special value to you, given your pending acquisition of U.S. Consumer Goods, is my expertise in managing all types of qualified retirement plans and nonqualified executive programs, meeting the combined needs of both the company and the employee.

In uniting U.S. Consumer Goods' plan with yours, my unique experience is essential to ensuring proper fiduciary compliance and accurate tax reporting in a regulatory environment as volatile as ours is today. I am adept at plan design, administration, and recordkeeping. I have worked closely with providers to enhance investment management and significantly improve cash flow and fund returns.

I'd like to discuss these and other ways in which I can bring you genuine effectiveness in your employee benefits program, and genuine cost-effectiveness to your bottom line.

Sincerely,

In this letter to a recruiter, the writer describes his experience clearly and convincingly. He also brings himself to life by including personality traits that suggest that he would be an interesting person to interview, which is not always the case and therefore can serve as an important advantage over other candidates.

LETTER 5-105   Corporate Trainer

Thank you for your time and the information you gave me during our phone conversation this morning. I have attached my resume, as you requested, and appreciate any leads to jobs that you can provide.

Permit me to summarize what is on my resume. My training experience covers <u>corporate personnel</u> (for PrimeFirst Bancorporation) as well as automotive industry <u>sales professionals</u> (for General Motors).

<u>I have effectively</u>:
- Conducted needs analyses.
- Designed specialized training programs.
- Designed classroom instruction curricula.
- Taught one-on-one.
- Created and administered a Management Development Program to support PrimeFirst's domestic operations.

> Lets his personality shine through.

I am outgoing and hardworking. My natural enthusiasm supports my ability to teach, inspire, and motivate others, from the entry-level trainee to participants in senior management training programs.

I will contact you shortly to see when we might get together. I look forward to discovering how I can assist your clients in achieving their training objectives.

Sincerely,

LETTER 5-106 Supply Chain Executive

In your search for an innovative Supply Chain Executive, I present my credentials, which match the qualities you seek—and then some. My resume, which is attached, illustrates that I am an experienced and highly skilled professional with an impressive record of achievement, catapulting growth while streamlining operations. Allow me to highlight additional strengths that other candidates may not offer:

- Extensive background in systems implementation, materials, procurement, and logistics.

- Lean Champion recognized for consistently surpassing SQDC metrics.

- Success in delivering strategic supply chain development for new market entry and product launches.

- Proven financial acumen, including P&L responsibility for annual budgets in excess of $20M.

- Recognized for negotiating advantageous supplier agreements through a rare blend of analytical and interpersonal skills.

- Proven TQM and JIT capabilities, leadership ability in cross-functional and multisite teams.

- Proficient in Hyperion Enterprise System, Logility Voyager, JDE OneWorld, JD Edwards, and SAP.

If you will contact me via phone or e-mail, I will be pleased to elaborate on my success in driving continuous improvement; enhancing operational efficiencies, lead time reduction, and cost containment; and boosting speed to market—all of which I look forward to contributing to your operations and bottom line.

LETTER 5-107 ▸ Management and Quality Training

RE: SimplyHired ad for Director, Management and Quality Training

To move forward powerfully, effectively, and rapidly, today's employees must align themselves with common goals and with common ways to achieve these goals.

Invariably, in promoting the concept of goal-oriented performance management, the organizations with which I have worked were pleased to discover that what's missing in many other quality initiatives is precisely what **I** have learned in more than 16 years of building high-performance teams. I have *combined* my methodology with the tools of quality and process management to create a synergy that is far superior to either approach standing alone.

As Director of your Management and Quality Training program, I will successfully lead your staff members to **challenge** the traditional *"not my job"* orientation. Instead, they will:

- **Adopt a broad view**, questioning and looking beyond existing methods of operating, in order to invest in the future.

- **Raise the overall level of their commitment** (despite setbacks, lack of support, and the passage of time) through the creation and nourishment of a **vision of quality.**

Forceful tone matches position.

The rewards are profound. The process is painless when you have the proper training and commitment at the helm. Let's get together so that we can discuss this in person.

LETTER 5-108 On-Staff Recruiter—Create an Opportunity—
Part-Time/Full-Time

Welcome to the neighborhood! Your move to White Plains from Long
Island will introduce your staff to a superb location full of exceptional
people—many of whom, in today's economic climate, may be available
to put their expertise to work for you.

Timely opening.

How will you find the best that this new area has to offer? What
Westchester publications will prove the most cost-effective for your
recruiting advertisements? What area headhunters and search firms
are the most reliable? Will your best on-staff recruiters be immediately available to interview in White Plains? How much will it cost you
to bring them in from Long Island, or send your candidates out there
for meetings?

The answer to all these questions is the same:

> **You'll save time and money by relying on a recruitment
> professional with solid experience, expertise, and contacts
> already in place right here in Westchester.**

As the attached resume illustrates, I have 12 years of recruiting background, much of it in this area—and I can put this to work for you
immediately. Whether on a consultant, part-time, or full-time basis,
I can serve as a valuable resource to help you get your new facility up
and running as quickly as possible.

> With the most qualified people.
> With minimum delay or misspent dollars.
> With maximum results.

Let's get together to discuss the difference I can make to your start-
up time. I'll give you a call to see if there's a convenient time for us to
meet. Or please feel free to call me at (555) 345-6789.

LETTER 5-109　Director, Human Resources and Administration— Career Change

RE: Director of Human Resources and Administrative Services

The position described in your ad seems to have been written for me. I have the precise qualifications you seek, and have been searching for just this opportunity to apply my business background to academic life.

Allow me to elaborate on the attached resume to demonstrate the strengths I can bring to your institution.

Human Resources Expertise. My employee relations responsibilities have made me skilled at conflict resolution, staffing, development, and personal counseling. For administrative hiring and staff recruiting, I develop position profiles, supervise onboarding/training and benefits administration, direct and provide input for employee evaluations and compensation, ensure legal compliance, and advance policy.

Administrative Expertise. Acting as the de facto Director of Administration, I supervise office and facilities services, marketing administration, and the research library. Because I have successfully directed projects involving the structuring and implementation of an online library "catalogue," office redesign, equipment planning and acquisition, marketing database design, and planning an e-newsletter, I can spearhead these and other initiatives on your behalf.

Exceptional Written Communication Skills. My ongoing work creating policy statements, project summaries, and e-newsletter and website content as well as presentations for myself and the company's senior management provides you with a valuable on-staff resource.

Throughout my successful career, I have maintained my connection to academia through my graduate studies in the sociology of education. The university environment is one in which I am well versed, challenged, and entirely comfortable.

I would welcome the opportunity to apply my skills and expertise in an academic setting such as yours. I offer you, in return, a colleague with the focus and ability to perform effectively under pressure— talents refined through 12 years in a fast-paced corporate setting.

LETTER 5-110 Director, Quality Management

The fact that you have advertised for a Quality Management Director demonstrates your commitment to realigning the corporate culture. It is this same commitment that has defined my career.

Indeed, over the past 25 years in corporate training and human resource development, my focus has been on supporting innovation and leadership—on actively designing rather than adapting to the future.

I am certain that my past achievements augur similar productivity improvements for Americana. For example, I have led corporate management teams to:

- Commit themselves entirely to the goal of superior quality in every aspect of service and performance.

- Drive this commitment into every level of the organization's culture and operations so that it becomes the everyday way of working.

- Free managers from their traditional focus on authority and control so that they can embrace critical leadership ideals.

- Build these transformations into an existing infrastructure, thus avoiding costly and time-consuming changes that erode success.

Undoubtedly, these are the objectives you seek to realize at Americana—and I would consider it a privilege to explore them further with you. I feel certain that my background and expertise (described in detail on the attached resume) would be a singular asset to your organization.

LETTER 5-111   Director, Productivity Improvement

In your search for a Director of Productivity Improvement, you are focusing on fostering, generating, expanding, and repeating results. *But first you have to find someone who has achieved these things.*

My resume presents my background and qualifications. Allow me to introduce myself through the results I have achieved. At Eagle Steel and DVC Equipment, I designed and implemented programs to foster breakthrough thinking. Learning to turn everyday obstacles and interruptions into innovation and success, our task teams:

- Increased both short- and long-term ROI by more than 38%.

- Improved cross-functional and cross-organizational teamwork by distinguishing *interpretation* from *fact* in order to take decisive actions.

- Realized quantum leaps in productivity performance, exceeding 80% in some cases, that went well beyond typical incremental improvements.

These are real, measurable, and profitable results. And they are reproducible at U.S. Manufacturing.

I'd like very much to meet with you in person. Please give me a call at (555) 765-4321. I'll alert my assistant to put your call through at once.

LETTER 5-112 Quality Engineer

In response to your CareerBuilder posting, I present my credentials and experience, which match ideally those you seek.

<u>I possess the knowledge you require.</u> Five years' experience and a Master's in Engineering. Fluency in word processing, spreadsheet, statistical, computer-aided drawing, and project scheduling software programs.

<u>I possess the skills you require.</u> Innovative and insightful. Able to handle multiple complex projects simultaneously, work under deadline pressure, and lead and mentor direct reports. Superior organizational talents as well as written and verbal communication, including the ability to present complex technical information clearly.

<u>I possess the professional qualifications you require.</u> Six Sigma Black Belt, ISO 13485, 9001 Auditor, Root Cause Analysis, and Systematic Corrective Action Qualifications.

<u>I possess the experience you require.</u>
- Close collaboration with design, manufacturing, engineering, and product management to identify opportunities for developing processes that increase productivity, reduce costs and time on task, enhance client satisfaction and overall effectiveness.
- Delivery of quality system guidance and training to ensure compliance with external regulatory standards, other engineering groups, and project teams.
- Protocol and report development, documentation review, and root cause investigation execution. Performance of risk and impact assessments for new products, equipment, testing, and process changes.
- Identification of work environment safety issues, solution recommendations, and implementation.
- Recognized ability to foster process buy-in by cultivating strong relationships at every level, from assembly-line workers to senior management and stakeholders.

There is no doubt that I am qualified and eager to assume responsibility for assuring that all quality activities are designed to build both products and processes that meet organizational objectives and fulfill customer satisfaction and ISO standards. May we have the chance to meet in person? I look forward to hearing from you.

A clever approach, appropriate for the industry and position, definitely attracts attention.

LETTER 5-113 ▶ **Chief Financial Officer**

Ms. Regina Lin, President
UniFex Corporation
18 Southern Parkway
Miami, Florida 09876

RE: Your ad for a CFO

Dear Ms. Lin:

You're looking at an actual demonstration of the results I can produce for you. At PSB, I've **expanded profit margins to 70%**. How? By cutting the cost of purchased goods by up to 25%. By cutting the cost of purchased services by up to 38%. By rigorously examining every expenditure to ensure maximum value at minimum cost. So why not hire me to do for UniFex what I do best? **I increase margins.** In fact, as you can see, I can't resist expanding any margin I can get my hands on.

Sincerely,

Richard C. Royce
(555) 456-7890

LETTER 5-114 Chief Financial Officer—Confidentiality

RE: TheLadders.com ad for a CFO

Yes, a Chief Financial Officer must be an expert in the administrative, financial, and risk management operations of the company—and I am. He or she must be fluent in developing a financial and operational strategy, monitoring and measuring its efficacy, directing the application and preservation of company assets, and reporting accurate financial results—and I am.

But the *superior* CFO has also produced the following results—as I have:

- Completely restructured business liability insurance to reduce costs by 15% and increase coverage.

- Doubled revenues in just 20 months by identifying, designing, and implementing accounting process improvements.

- Directed successful due diligence for 15+ global and domestic acquisitions, from pipeline development to postacquisition integration and metrics.

- Increased margins by 275 basis points in five months by correcting pricing errors; augmented cash flow by $900K by streamlining accounts receivable and inventory levels.

This is simply an overview of my most recent accomplishments. It should demonstrate the commitment I make to cost control and heightened return. Yes, I am currently employed and would appreciate your confidentiality when contacting me, but I'm pleased to make myself available to meet at your convenience.

LETTER 5-115 ▸ Managing Director

From forging global strategy to understanding the challenges faced by line workers, the demands on your firm's top leader are extraordinary. You need a proven, results-driven executive who thinks critically, negotiates adroitly, fosters loyalty, and deploys deep industry knowledge to create revenue-generating opportunities. Someone with a record of cultivating ownership of enterprise-wide initiatives in order to meet and exceed objectives. Someone who promotes personal and professional achievement at every level of the organization.

These are the credentials I've developed throughout my 20-year career building profitability, productivity, and visibility at both start-ups and established firms, where I had singular responsibility for the following select accomplishments, among others:

- Turnaround of a $15M clothing designer that resulted in emergence from Chapter 11 and return to profitability within two years.

- Increase of 110 basis points in a textile manufacturer's profitability through redesign of its pricing model and global human resource redeployment.

- Successful direction of an e-transformation project for a $MM global hardware manufacturer, including strategic program development, resource management, and financial analysis.

As this is but "the tip of the iceberg" and there is so much more to discuss, I welcome your inquiries and interest. I can be reached at (123) 456-7890 or, of course, by return e-mail.

LETTER 5-116 Cybersecurity Engineer/Analyst

For cybersecurity professionals, life's never been more exciting. Information security evolves daily. Organizations (and hackers) function in a complex, dynamic operating environment. Our job—to reveal intelligence, maintain security, manage risk, and strengthen resilience—is a challenging one . . . and exhilarating!

With more than eight years' experience in information security, I am trained (BS, Information Systems), certified (CISSP), and skilled at deploying the following tools, systems, and services: intrusion detection/prevention, firewall and server audit log monitoring, vulnerability assessment and alerts, technical compliance monitoring, security event and incident management, and cloud security. (The attached resume contains a full list of my qualifications.)

As a result, I can assure a proactive approach to monitoring cyberthreats; provide expertise and advice on threat risk and business impact; conduct comprehensive digital forensics; and build, implement, and deploy data security solutions.

> **The result for you? Safeguarded information systems.**
> **Protected data. Productive operations. Satisfied clients.**
> **Sound, secure reputation.**

I hope you'll contact me so that we can discuss further the exciting possibility of my bringing my expertise to your organization.

LETTER 5-117   Cloud Infrastructure Engineer

For everyone in IT, Apple is IT—the number one place to work. Unlike everyone in IT, however, I offer Apple an uncommon blend of strengths, talents, and proficiencies in response to your job posting for a Cloud Infrastructure Engineer.

As you'll see on the attached resume, my background equips me ideally to build next-gen infrastructure for current and forthcoming Apple innovations. I am fluent in the exact areas the position requires: AWS, OpenStack, Eucalyptus, and configuration management tools such as Puppet. I can work in Python, Perl, Ruby, and Shell Script development environments. I'm experienced at developing written procedures, engineering drawings, and other technical documentation. I enjoy troubleshooting, as it keeps my skills sharp and my mind open to new approaches. My passion is to achieve the level of deep technical expert and thought leader in cloud computing, a goal I'm well on my way to realizing.

I believe my skills, enthusiasm, commitment, and drive reflect Apple's exceptional standards. May we meet, either virtually or actually, so that I can convince you of the benefits I can offer you? I look forward to it.

Best regards,

CHAPTER 6

The Follow-Up Letter

How Follow-Up Letters Differ from Thank You Letters

Before you read any further, it's imperative that you understand the distinction between the Follow-Up Letter, which is covered in *this* chapter, and the Thank You Letter, which is covered in the *following* chapter. In a Thank You Letter, your *sole* purpose for writing is to express appreciation. In the Follow-Up Letter, your "thank you" is only an *excuse* for writing to someone who has the power either to hire you or to influence the hiring decision in your favor.

In this chapter, we focus on the follow-up letter, the letter or e-mail that you send after being interviewed for a position that you are interested in attaining. Although you may begin your follow-up letter by thanking your reader for a meeting, advice, a referral, or consideration, your *primary goal* is to continue promoting yourself and your candidacy. You accomplish this by achieving your *secondary goal*, which is to strengthen the connection with your reader that you established during an interview, meeting, or other prior contact.

When should you send a follow-up letter after interviewing for a position in which you are interested? Always. When should you send the same person another follow-up letter after interviewing a second time for a position in which you are interested? Always. When should you send a follow-up letter after receiving help from someone who can influence the hiring decision? Always.

You'll find follow-up letters easy to draft if you follow these steps.

Step 1: Reestablish the Connection

Open your letter or e-mail by mentioning something that will identify you to your reader, such as the time or place of the meeting. Because it's likely that your prospective employer has met with numerous candidates, it's vital that she remembers you. If your meeting occurred early in the hiring process, it's even more critical that your interviewer remembers you. And it's vital that her memory of you is a positive one.

Therefore, in your opening, refer to a common link that was revealed during your meeting. You may have discovered, for example, that you and your interviewer both worked at the same company in the past, or that you share an alma mater, professional association, or business philosophy. Such a connection subtly suggests that you and your prospective employer are similar in some way, and that you will find common ground on which to build a rapport. (Unless you're planning to work for Scrooge himself, it's a sure bet that your next boss will be searching for someone with whom he or she can get along on a daily basis.)

If there is no apparent connection of this type, refer to an unusual topic you discussed with your interviewer, or something you believe may be of interest or importance to whomever you're writing.

Sample Openings

- I enjoyed our lunch at the River Club, and I thank you for your interest in me.
- It was a pleasure meeting you on Monday, and I appreciate the time you spent with me.

RECRUITER'S TIP > An Interview to Remember

Interviewing in the office of your prospective employer affords you an unbeatable opportunity. Scan the room for photographs, trophies, awards, or diplomas. If it's on display, it probably represents something positive to its owner. Use this as a point of discussion that you can refer to later on in your follow-up. It will help you establish a personal connection that your competition may not share—and make you more memorable to your interviewer.

- Our meeting last week was very valuable for me, and I appreciate your willingness to fit me into your busy schedule.
- It was a pleasure meeting you again yesterday to discuss the opening in your media department. I especially appreciate your willingness to meet me so early in the morning.
- Thank you for your time last Friday. It was a pleasure discussing the plans you've conceived for your sales team, and I would welcome the opportunity to develop new business for your division.
- Meeting with you Tuesday morning was invaluable to me. It was rewarding to discover that a fellow U.S. Iron veteran has penetrated the upper echelons of our industry. Working with you would be a privilege.
- Thank you for your time at our breakfast on the 14th. I enjoyed meeting you, and swapping mountain bike trail secrets. Perhaps our paths will cross on Mt. Boulder; I certainly hope they will cross in business.
- I appreciate the time you spent with me on the 26th and the information you provided on Data International's growth strategies. It was heartening to learn that we share the same excitement regarding the future of our industry, a future in which I hope to play an important role.
- Thank you for your time this past Wednesday morning. I enjoyed meeting with you again and comparing HydroMat stories. Our combined experiences certainly represent the good, the bad, and the ugly!

RECRUITER'S TIP > **To Be . . . or Not to Be: Manager or Recruiter?**

Few of the people with whom you'll meet will be trained recruiters or skilled interviewers. They are simply managers with a position to fill. A strong follow-up letter can help them accomplish the following:

- Narrow their choices.
- Match your skills to their needs.
- Let them know that you're still available.

And get back to work!

- I am grateful to you for introducing me to your colleagues. Meeting Mr. Simon and Ms. Weiss has only enhanced my desire to put my strengths to work on your behalf. I would be thrilled to join the impressive legal team you've built.
- Thank you for introducing me to Jim Williams. As you predicted, he offered me a wealth of advice. I'm grateful for his perspective and for your interest.

Step 2: Inform

You may notice that this step is the same as Step 2 in your resume cover letters. That's because in both situations, your letter is dedicated to promoting your candidacy. To do so, you must sell both your strengths and the benefits they will bring your next employer.

In the body of your letter, remind your reader of the skills or knowledge you have that make you perfectly suited to fill the open position. But don't stop with that—as your competition will.

Link these qualities to the meaningful advantages that they offer your next boss and her company. To do this, think of your unique attributes as falling into four categories: profits, productivity, performance, and personal satisfaction. Ask yourself how you can contribute to the success of the organization or firm, a specific division, a team of people, or your immediate supervisor. Will your skills help to enhance productivity? Will your past achievements equip you to help increase future profits? Will you add to or improve performance metrics? Will your personal satisfaction contribute in some way, such as boosting morale, setting an example, or introducing new ideas or a new perspective? You'll find that the most important benefits you can deliver will involve one or more of these areas.

In the body of your follow-up letter, you might also supply additional references or more detailed information on your skills. You might clarify or strengthen comments made during an interview.

If you are attempting to overcome a problem that was raised in your interview, provide a clear explanation with valid support points—not excuses! A good illustration is provided in Follow-Up Letter 6-1. In this case, the writer had traveled to Denver to interview for a position in which she was very interested. Later, thinking back on the meeting, she became discouraged. Although she was more than willing to relocate for the job, she worried that her interviewer may have regarded the fact that she was from out of town as a drawback—a problem that she did not perceive or address at the time. Instead of giving up, however, she responded with significant assurances that she could relocate successfully, building contacts and business relationships as she has done before.

LETTER 6-1 Follow-Up Letter—Insurance Sales—Relocation

Thank you for spending so much time with me during my visit to your headquarters on Monday.

Seeing the respect that was evident between you and your colleagues was completely refreshing for me—as was discovering the innovative sales strategies that you've introduced. I am eager to join forces with you.

> Dispels concerns raised during interview.

You can count on me to quickly become a familiar face to prospects, clients, and business leaders in and around Denver. Through previous moves, I have become adept at forging contacts and friendships through my personal interest in the arts as well as my participation in the activities of local business groups (such as the Lifers Club, United Way, Police Athletic League, Financial Marketing Association, Advertising Club, and the Red Cross in Atlanta). Turning these connections into sales is integral to my status as the top biller at my agency for four years running.

I will forward additional information to you shortly to support what my record has already proven: that I will produce nothing less than outstanding results for you and Long Life.

Sincerely,

Step 3: Instruct

It can be beneficial to include a reference to what will happen next in the hiring process—even if it's simply that you will wait to be contacted. Clarifying this can help avoid misunderstandings about who will take the next step.

If the next step will be his or hers, *describe your understanding of what the reader will do*. Be sure to provide a complete address, e-mail address, and telephone number at which you can be reached, stating whether the number is for work, home, or a mobile phone. As you did in your Resume Cover Letter, let your reader know if you prefer to be called during certain hours and if confidentiality is an issue.

If you will be the one to take the next step, *tell the reader what to expect*. You may make a general reference, such as, "I'll call you shortly." Or you may be specific about what, when, and how you'll follow up: by phone, e-mail, Skype, or some other avenue or action. If you know that the hiring process has just begun, inform the reader that you'll call to follow up in two weeks, ten days, or whenever you feel it's appropriate.

Attaching supplemental material to your follow-up letter or e-mail always requires an explanation. Describe what is in the attachment: an updated resume, a list of accomplishments, references, a link to your website, or other information.

If you will be sending something to the reader, such as a letter of reference, explain what it is and when and how it should arrive.

Optional Step 4: Close Warmly

A strong, yet warm closing line leaves your reader with a positive impression.

When appropriate, lighthearted, friendly, and even personal sign-offs are also acceptable and advisable. You might make a personal reference or mention something about the reader that suggests that he is not receiving a form letter, but rather getting a letter that was written specifically to him. If you are on a first-name basis with your reader, you might add the reader's name to your closing. A warm ending to your message makes you seem friendly and approachable, and indicates that you are the kind of person with whom most of us would prefer to work.

> **RECRUITER'S TIP** > **Thorough Follow-Through**
>
> After an interview, follow-through on your part is critical. The person to whom you're writing may not scrutinize every word in your follow-up letter, but he or she will surely notice that you've sent one—and be impressed that you did!
>
> Plus, a good recruiter will expect to hear from you on the precise day you promised to follow up—so do so. Without fail.

How do you gauge the right tone? Generally, the degree of warmth you add should correspond with the number of times you've met your reader—without ever crossing the line by getting too personal or being rude. Use your judgment; do what you feel comfortable with—but by all means, don't choose *not* to close your letter because you don't feel like writing a closing line.

Here are some sample closings for the follow-up letter that may inspire you!

Sample Closings

- Thank you for your time and consideration.
- I appreciate your assistance.
- I thank you again for your time and candor. Let's talk again soon!
- Thank you for the opportunity to pursue the position of Research Director.
- I look forward to our next meeting.
- I look forward to seeing you again, Randy, on the tennis courts and at headquarters.
- I am eager to continue our discussions.
- My best wishes for your continued success in the year ahead.
- My best wishes for another successful quarter for your team.
- I would welcome the chance to work with you.
- Bill, I would consider it a privilege to join forces with you and hope to hear from you shortly.
- I would welcome the opportunity to contribute to your firm, and I look forward to speaking with you soon.
- I have no doubt that my past success is a preview of what I can produce for you and for MicroTech. I look forward to speaking with you soon.

Samples

LETTER 6-2 Follow-Up Letter—Bank Operations Manager

Thank you for allowing me to present myself as a candidate for Operations Manager, a prospect about which I am very excited. It was a pleasure meeting you on Wednesday—and discovering our mutual midwestern roots!

Given my background, I can understand the need for a manager who can attend to detail without compromising the division's overall profitability. Throughout my tenure with Fidelity, I have worked to achieve these demanding goals. During the past 10 years, I personally led the division to cut costs by 36% while improving our overall accuracy rate to 98%.

What this means for you is that as Constitution's Operations Manager, I can bring the same skill, insight, and experience to motivate your staff to improve accuracy, streamline costs, and increase the effectiveness of the "back room," bringing operations to the forefront of the bank's profit centers.

I will contact you shortly to see when we might meet again to expand upon this vital goal.

Reaffirms connection.

Informs by providing a benefit that is meaningful to the employer.

Instructs how the next step will occur.

When her interview was unexpectedly cut short, this candidate arranged to complete it the next day via Skype. She used this unusual situation to remind the reader of their meeting and then continued with an upbeat tone.

LETTER 6-3 Follow-Up Letter—Attorney

I'm so pleased we were able to continue our discussions via Skype, and I thank you for your time.

As you can tell, I am very excited about the opportunity to work with you and the top-notch team you've developed at Gencliffe, Ackerman, and Hahn. I am particularly inspired by your belief in the value of promoting from within, which seems to be a rare insight these days. For this reason, and to provide further proof of the unique talents I can bring to your team, I have enclosed a summary of my recent case findings.

I am eager to prove my abilities to you on a firsthand basis. I will keep in touch to see when we might meet again, and if there is any other information I can provide you in the meantime.

Thank you again for your time and consideration.

LETTER 6-4 ▶ Follow-Up Letter—Medical Research and Design

Aids recall.

Thank you for your time during our luncheon last week. My journey from Conshohocken to Reading was a breeze, just as you predicted!

VisionQuest's innovations are legendary, and it was fascinating to discover the efforts that went into your unique achievements. Those who benefit from your firm's breakthrough technologies in nonsurgical visual impairment treatments cannot imagine the dedication and training required of your teams.

I would welcome the opportunity to join a team such as yours and have, therefore, attached a summary of my own accomplishments in research and design. Because my procedures and standards of measurement are so similar to those employed by VisionQuest, my assimilation with your team's methodology would be quite smooth—a breeze, in fact, like my trip to Reading!

Please let me know what additional information I can provide to help sway your hiring decision in my direction. I thank you again for your time.

Another example of ingenuity following an interrupted interview. Enclosing a photo is unusual... exactly why it will attract attention!

LETTER 6-5 Follow-Up Letter—Sales/Marketing

It was a pleasure meeting you during my visit to Albany, and I look forward to the opportunity to continue our discussion.

After a delightful and very informative lunch with Susan Camelitto, I am tremendously excited by the prospect of working in the challenging and highly creative environment you've established. In return, I will bring you my proven strengths in research and new business development.

As our meeting was cut short, I have taken the liberty of enclosing my picture so that I'm clearly in your mind until we meet again, and I can convince you that I'm the ideal addition to your team.

Sincerely,

LETTER 6-6 Follow-Up Letter—IT—Sales

Thank you for your time on Wednesday. Our discussion left me even more excited about your sales team—and convinced that I'd be a perfect fit.

As you know, I have dedicated the last 10 years of my career to systems engineering and administration. Now I'm eager to make that same commitment to a promising start-up—as Manning Technologies is.

Hire me, and you'll get a loyal employee who works hard and smart, thrives in a high-energy, fast-paced environment, and understands how to deliver end-to-end business solutions for the enterprise and middle-market sectors. You'll get someone with an established, solid reputation who will add to your image *and* your bottom line.

Arthur, I look forward to building big things together.

LETTER 6-7 ▸ *Follow-Up Letter—Supply Chain Management*

Reaffirms
connection.

I enjoyed our meeting last week and appreciate your time and candor. As another ex-Hewlett-Packard employee, your perspective was especially meaningful to me.

My decade of experience in supply chain management has made me a planner, a promoter, and a problem solver—and it is a real pleasure to meet someone who values these qualities. Joining a division that recognizes and depends upon these strengths provides precisely the environment and challenge that I seek.

In return, I offer you my <u>proven</u> record of improving efficiency and reducing costs, exceeding revenue goals and meeting budget objectives, improving forecast accuracy, strengthening working capital, and ensuring raw materials and manpower availability—all of which my superiors will verify as my references!

I'd welcome the opportunity to work with you and will be in contact to see how we can make this happen.

The Case of the Poor Interviewer: although this candidate could tell that the employer was impressed with her qualifications, she also surmised that he didn't know how best to make use of her skills. So she gives him several ideas.

LETTER 6-8 ▸ Follow-Up Letter—General

Thank you for the time you so generously spent with me this afternoon.

Now that I know so much more about NetworCorp's varied activities, I am even more eager to be a part of the company's future. Certainly, your firm and I both thrive on creativity, innovation, and the energy of the entrepreneur and the deal maker.

For this reason, as I mentioned during our meeting, I hope that you will think of me should an opportunity arise. Whether it is sales or marketing, dealing with the largest advertisers or new business development, or working abroad or as your right-hand man, I would welcome the chance to work with you.

I thank you again for your time and consideration.

LETTER 6-9 ▶ Follow-Up Letter—General

Meeting you today was a real pleasure. I enjoyed touring your facility and seeing a staff that collaborates so seamlessly to achieve impressive productivity. Quite a departure from the typical corporate environment!

As we discussed, the position is an exciting one for which I am superbly qualified, and it would be an honor to join your team. The range of skills I can bring to your organization would allow your managers to devote more time to joint fieldwork, and ultimately increase your bottom-line profits.

Employer benefits.

I will call on Friday as you suggested to see whether Roger Transwood has returned and is available to meet with me.

Thank you again for your time. I look forward to seeing you again very soon.

LETTER 6-10   Follow-Up Letter—Security

It was a pleasure speaking with you recently about your plans to expand into Asia's corporate market.

I am anxious to pursue our discussion of the exciting profit potential that such a program can offer your firm—a potential of which I am well aware, having built Wytech Security's South American program from the ground up to its current status as a major profit center for the company.

As a springboard for this discussion, I have attached my updated resume, as my responsibilities have recently increased. I now lead the planning and implementation of one of the company's major strategic initiatives: promoting multisite security systems throughout the Americas. I am responsible for the sale of full-service security system packages, which include customized system design, installation, and staff training.

As a result, I can deliver the experience, foresight, and personal contacts required to tap Asia's corporate security market and to take full advantage of its potential for return.

I will contact you again shortly to see how we might proceed. I thank you again for your consideration and look forward to seeing you.

LETTER 6-11 ▸ Follow-Up Letter—Student

Thank you for speaking with me at the recent State Collegiate Career Fair. Our conversation made a striking impression on me, and I appreciate your interest and encouragement.

As we discussed, I have attached my resume as a follow-up to our discussion. Allow me to provide this brief overview of what I can offer your firm:

Leadership: Student Government Vice President, Sorority President, and Big Sister Volunteer while maintaining a 3.5 GPA.

Interpersonal Strengths: I am pleased to report that my colleagues describe me as a go-getter who is reliable, pleasant, encouraging, and loyal.

Drive: I will be available to begin work immediately upon receiving my BS in Business Administration this spring from State University.

I will be in the area again next month, and will call to set up an appointment. In the meantime, I thank you again for your time at the Career Fair, and look forward to meeting you again soon.

LETTER 6-12   Follow-Up Letter—Bookkeeper

Thank you for the opportunity to interview for the Bookkeeper position. Hearing you recount the growth your company has enjoyed, I am certain that your own hard work and commitment are the roots of your success.

As your bookkeeper, I will bring the same dedication to the fulfillment of your firm's accounting responsibilities.

- I am adept at handling all aspects of your accounts payable, accounts receivable, payroll, and payroll taxes. My five years of experience in these areas means that you can rely on me for skill and accuracy.

- Unlike others in my field, I am well versed in handling a payroll with diverse commissions and bonus structures. This reduces or eliminates the potential for problems that arise when payment errors aggravate your sales representatives.

- Furthermore, my technological proficiency (Peachtree, MAS90, and QuickBooks for Mac) allows me to contribute immediately, without taking valuable company time for training.

I would very much like to join your firm. If you require any additional information before making your decision, please let me know. I would be pleased to visit your office again for another meeting or provide further references, if you wish.

In her interview, this candidate picked up on the importance her prospective boss placed on a single qualification: the ability to deal with difficult people. She focused on this here, even providing additional references to support her claim.

LETTER 6-13   Follow-Up Letter—Assistant Buyer

It was wonderful speaking with you last week. Thank you for spending so much time with me.

I am extremely interested in pursuing the Assistant Buyer opening at your firm because it represents the perfect match between your needs and my strengths.

My retailing background has familiarized me with an industry in which diplomacy and tact are of supreme importance. As we discussed, the ability to assess an individual quickly in order to respond appropriately and productively is more a personality trait than an acquired skill—it can rarely be taught.

Great idea!

I am pleased to report that my colleagues have repeatedly acknowledged my abilities in interpersonal communications. In fact, I invite you to check my LinkedIn profile to view recommendations from colleagues and clients on this very topic.

I hope it is evident that I would welcome the chance to work for Valentin Designs with you personally, Mr. Valentin. Please let me know if there is any further information you require.

Like its predecessor, Cover Letter 5-87, this letter is heartfelt and sincere, yet still informative—very effective.

LETTER 6-14   Follow-Up Letter—Teaching Artist

Thank you for taking an interest in me as a teaching artist for Lincoln Center. I enjoyed our conversation last week, and have received the information you forwarded to me.

This position represents an important opportunity for me to continue my productive association with the Lincoln Center Institute. As both a dancer and a dance captain with LCI, I meet regularly with the artists prior to our performances to explore the link between the classroom material and the postperformance open talk. Invariably, this preparation proves priceless to students, who benefit from a newfound familiarity with the elements of dance and the terminology introduced in class.

This, along with my current participation as a member of your affiliated New York City Baroque Dance Company, reinforces my teaching philosophy: to share with my students the great joy of movement. I have found that every student can experience the pleasures of dancing, and of learning about the many methods for expression through movement. Depending upon their age and level, I introduce my students to various technical challenges, dance forms, and elements of composition. With the advantage of live performance, which your program offers, a teacher can guide the students toward a better understanding and appreciation of the performing arts. Books, pictures, and video can enhance, but not replace, the experience of a live performance—and the students truly enjoy it!

As an artist, I believe we have an obligation to show society the ways in which art can be brought into the mainstream of education. As a mother, I understand that a child's intellectual and emotional development must be well rounded. I feel strongly that we can allow neither politics nor family dysfunction to affect an entire new generation adversely. We owe it to future artists to help create a society that is supportive of the arts, one in which the arts may flourish.

Combined, my experience and commitment offer the advantages that only a dedicated artist and educator can offer. I would appreciate the opportunity to meet with you personally. I salute the wonderful LCI program, and thank you again for your consideration.

LETTER 6-15   Follow-Up Letter—Pharmaceuticals— Technical Writer

---

Congratulations on your promotion! It's so gratifying to see women recognized for their skills.

I enjoyed speaking with you on the phone yesterday, and with this note, I am forwarding information on myself and my capabilities. As you'll see, I've had a fair amount of experience within the financial services arena as well as a pseudo-medical education.

My particular expertise is in the pharmaceuticals industry, a field in which many writers are less fluent. I am well versed in the chemical and medical terminology that supports a vast range of pediatric, nutritional, pharmaceutical, and nutriceutical prescriptions and over-the-counter products, as well as the regulations governing their discussion in any public forum. This knowledge allows me to execute a greater number of projects at a far faster pace than other technical writers.

I would welcome the chance to show you samples of my work, at your convenience. When things settle down for both of us, let's get together. I will call you again toward the end of this month.

In the meantime, I wish you the best in your new position.

LETTER 6-16 Follow-Up Letter—Medical Research—Job Loss

It was great to see you and reminisce about our days at Growth Systems. Seems like just yesterday—but I digress!

Although I am chagrined that Genebyte's hiring freeze is still in place, I do appreciate your offer to recommend me after the thaw. As you know, our work at Growth Systems during the early days of stem cell research affords us a background that few can match. It would be a thrill to join forces with you again—especially on a project as exciting as your human genome initiative.

Hal, thanks again for seeing me and filling me in on Genebyte's activities. Please give my regards to Jill.

I'll keep in touch.

LETTER 6-17   Follow-Up Letter—Fund-Raising/Development

Thank you so much for your time today discussing the possibility of my joining the University development team. It is clear from our talking (and my learning) that the school is in a state of uneasy transition, and yet also, and more important, is prepared to raise significant funding to strengthen and support its primary mission to "prepare tomorrow's leaders to shape a just and humane society."

All that is needed now is the right person for the job—someone who is qualified to cultivate confidence and earn the trust of her colleagues and constituency, who is genuine in her support of the school and persuasive in generating substantial and ongoing financial support, with the drive to succeed in positioning the University to thrive in the years ahead.

Of course, I would like to think that I have those qualities! To the extent that I do not, however, I am certain that I could develop them under your able leadership. For these reasons, I remain both intrigued by and keenly interested in joining your development team.

In the interests of full disclosure, I want you to know that I do have two interviews lined up this week for other positions in the field, but I will look forward to hearing from you in the days and weeks ahead regarding next steps in the process. In the meantime, please let me know if you have any questions or concerns.

CHAPTER 7

The Thank You Letter

Note: Before you proceed any further into this chapter than this paragraph, be sure you are reading the appropriate material. The Thank You Letter and the Follow-Up Letter are entirely different from each other. Each is written and sent under completely different circumstances. If you have just concluded an interview and wish to send a letter to promote your candidacy further, turn back to Chapter 6 for instructions on how to compose a Follow-Up Letter. If you wish to send a brief, yet sincere, note of appreciation—and you have no hidden agenda—read on.

When to Send a Thank You Letter

Thank you letters are honest and straightforward, with a simple, singular message. Your only reason for writing is to say "thank you," and nothing else. You may be expressing your gratitude to someone for an introduction, advice, a referral, or serving as a reference for you. You may have interviewed for a job that you do not intend to pursue, but wish to thank your interviewer for seeing you.

These are the circumstances that occasion writing and sending a thank you letter, and effective jobhunters never overlook them. In fact, you should actively seek opportunities to send thank you notes. The reason is simple: people like to be appreciated. Doing something for someone else involves going out of our way, and we feel (rightly) that we deserve acknowledgment for it. If we give nothing more than our time, we've given a great deal, as time is, invariably, in short supply. When you satisfy this need to be appreciated, you help cement a positive image of yourself in your reader's mind—one that will serve you well should you ever approach this person with another request. And in today's complex, connected, interactive business environment, you will. Not only are you highly likely to have additional contact with your reader, but successful networking depends upon it. Do not miss an opportunity to send a thank you note—you may be repaid with unexpected surprises later on!

At its most basic, a thank you letter is an expression of feelings. These e-mails, letters, and notes should be short, and, contrary to popular belief, they are easy to write as long as you state your message simply. Your *primary goal* is to thank someone for her time, assistance, or support. You should have *no secondary goal*; if you do, it's likely that the letter you should be writing is a Follow-up Letter (see Chapter 6) or a Make Something Happen Letter (see Chapter 8).

Step 1: State the Occasion

Open your letter by referring to the occasion that inspired it. Tell the reader why you're writing. Be clear, direct, and brief. A few examples follow; you'll find plenty more in the sample letters in this chapter.

Sample Openings

- Thank you for your time and advice.
- Thank you for seeing me yesterday.
- Your time and advice are most appreciated, and I thank you for meeting with me.
- Knowing how busy you are at this time of year, I am grateful that you were able to make the time to meet with me.

RECRUITER'S TIP > **Berate the Belated**

Thank you letters should be short, direct, and easier to compose than other jobhunting letters—so there's no excuse for delaying sending them.

Always send your letter within one or two days of whatever occasion you're acknowledging.

If you can't meet this deadline, send a letter whenever you can, even weeks after the fact. It's never too late to thank someone for a kindness.

- Thank you for fitting me into your busy schedule. I appreciate the suggestions you made regarding my search for work and have already begun to contact the organizations you recommended. I appreciate your willingness to help me in my job search and thank you for passing my name along to your associates.
- Thank you for serving as a reference for me in my job search. Your recommendation will prove most valuable, as your name is so highly regarded in our field.
- Thank you for introducing me to Dr. Beatty. I appreciate your assistance and the referral to such an outstanding professional.

Step 2: Provide Information or State Your Feelings

The body of your letter is the place to provide a bit of detail. This is where you'll tell your reader *how* his or her assistance was valuable to you.

Be specific about what you are thanking your readers for; if they don't know you personally, they may have already forgotten you! Make your thanks meaningful to the person who helped you—if the results of that help were positive, mention them and the difference they made in your job search. Say, for example, that a colleague recommended that you contact a Ms. Farrell. You called her, scheduled a get-together, and gained important advice during the meeting. Because your colleague will want to know how you used the referral and how the meeting went, you might write:

> Meeting Ms. Farrell was invaluable to me. She shared with me her view of the future of endocrine therapy research, which in turn, led me to refine my job search strategy. As a result of our meeting, I will be contacting Stan Whitmore, an acquaintance of Ms. Farrell's, who directs product development for Pfizer Inc.'s pharmaceutical division.

Not only is it a courtesy to inform your colleague of the results of the referral, but it's good networking. With the knowledge that you have handled the referral properly (and that Ms. Farrell found you impressive enough to refer you to one of her own colleagues), your friend is likely to be willing to provide additional assistance in the future. (It should go without saying that the next letter you write will be to Ms. Farrell.)

If you choose not to go into this level of detail—for example, if the results were less than you expected—state your feelings instead of providing information. In this case, the rule is always: say—don't describe—how you feel. Whether you're mildly grateful, very grateful, eternally grateful, or not at all grateful, this can be accomplished in very few words. Give the necessary information and *stop*.

Your thank you letters should always be brief, direct, and written with a positive tone of voice. Because they are short and easy to write, there's no excuse for avoiding sending a thank you letter. So don't pass up this chance to network! Use the sample letters provided on the following pages to guide you as you compose your own.

Samples

LETTER 7-1 Thank You for Time and Contact—
Marketing/Advertising—Social Media

Gracias! Merci! Danke schoen! Thank you! In any language, my appreciation is genuine. You gave me your time and your expert advice this past Tuesday, and I am very grateful.

States occasion.

You reassured me that despite tough times in the ad business, opportunities do exist for those who are willing to create them—and social media seems to be THE place to start. Thanks to my experience in targeting niche markets, I am ideally equipped to tap new markets and build user engagement to build the kind of trust and familiarity that will ultimately drive sales, especially online and globally.

How it helped.

Your suggestion to contact Victor Morelli is much appreciated. I have just e-mailed him my resume; I hope to discuss with him Victory Advertising's international plans, to which, I am certain, I can contribute fresh ideas, valuable experience, and strategic insight.

With sincerest thanks,

LETTER 7-2   Thank You for Contact—General

Thank you for forwarding my resume to William Ford.

Mr. Ford has contacted me, and we plan to meet on Tuesday, March 5. Our brief telephone conversation assures me that he will be a valuable resource in my job search.

I will call you next week to let you know the details of our meeting.

I appreciate your efforts on my behalf.

LETTER 7-3   Thank You for Referral—Legal

Thank you for referring me to Bill Hancock at Manhattan Legal Services.

Mr. Hancock contacted me today, and we have scheduled a meeting for next Wednesday, the 17th of April.

I couldn't have been more pleased when he indicated that it was you who referred me to him. My sincerest thanks for thinking of me, and making the time for an introduction. You have become a valuable resource in my job search, and I am grateful for all you have done.

I will let you know the results of my meeting with Mr. Hancock.

With best regards,

LETTER 7-4 ▶ **Thank You for Consideration**

Thank you for your time and interest during our meeting last week. American Products' planned expansion into South American and African markets is as fascinating as it is challenging.

While the opportunity to participate in this exciting new venture is extremely appealing, I must, unfortunately, withdraw my name from consideration. I had hoped to be able to accept an international assignment, but I have recently been offered additional responsibilities in my current position, which will also involve limited travel overseas.

Nonetheless, I want to thank you for allowing me to explore what promises to be a career-making opportunity for the executive fortunate enough to be selected.

Meeting you was a pleasure, and I will stay in touch. My best wishes for your continued success.

LETTER 7-5 ▶ **Thank You for Reference**

I have just returned from my second interview with Phyllis Anderson at Anderson, Wilton, and Slatsky. She was thrilled with your comments about my performance during my tenure with you at DPC International—and so am I!

As you know, I am anxious to further my career, and working with Ms. Anderson will supplement my experience in a meaningful and productive way.

I am so grateful to you for providing me with a positive recommendation. One day the opportunity will arise for me to repay your kindness, and you can be certain that I will do exactly that with great enthusiasm.

In the meantime, my deepest thanks.

This is a lovely thank you note that sets the stage should this student decide to contact the reader again later in the networking process.

LETTER 7-6   Thank You for Advice—Student

I cannot let another day pass without letting you know how very valuable I found your Jobhunting Seminar at North Carolina University last month. Your suggestions, ideas, and tips were very enlightening, and I have already put them to use in my job search.

Of greatest benefit for many of us was the motivation you sparked. Continuing the search can be especially daunting for students, who are competing with the hundreds of thousands of graduates flooding the market each spring, not to mention the many Americans already looking for work.

I shall remember your advice every day until I have successfully secured employment—when I hope to have the chance to pass it along to other students graduating in the years to come.

Best regards,

Before this contact, this jobhunter wrote her professor to ask whether he would serve as a reference. That letter appears in Chapter 9. (See Letter 9-1.)

LETTER 7-7   Thank You for Reference—Student

I owe you dual thanks: first, for serving as a reference for me to aid in my job search, and second, for your kind words.

I have just heard from John Brunswick at St. Louis Federal, and Leslie Rubin at the South County Credit Union. They both informed me that you offered high praise of my work and my attitude.

As a result of your recommendations, I have been invited to join South County's training program. I should learn my status at St. Louis Federal shortly, and you can be certain that I will contact you as soon as I receive this decision.

So, for your dual role in my search, I thank you once, and I thank you again.

Friends and family deserve recognition just as much as business colleagues do. The only difference is that a thank you letter such as this one (which is written to the mother of a high school buddy) may be handwritten on personal notepaper, if you choose. An alternative is to use a more casual or script font in an e-mail.

LETTER 7-8   Thank You for Contact—General

Thank you for introducing me to your brother, Charles Armour. I spoke with his Administrative Assistant just this morning and have scheduled a meeting for next Wednesday at his Maple Shade plant!

Armour Development has such a fine reputation in our area. I am looking forward to touring your brother's facilities and gaining the benefit of any advice he may offer in my job search.

Mrs. Gold, it was so kind of you to help me. I truly appreciate your interest. Just as when Tom and I were playing football for the high school, you're still cheering us on! That support means a lot. Thank you.

Fondly,

LETTER 7-9   Thank You for Time and Contact—General

Just a note to thank you for a most enjoyable early Monday morning meeting. It was nice meeting you and then seeing you again later at the CPG outing!

Now that I know more about your organization's objectives and opportunities, I am excited about the potential for reaching new segments of the market. I appreciate your willingness to have me meet your colleague, Frank Harley, a meeting I have arranged for next Wednesday.

Your offer to call with any questions that may arise is a kind one, and I will surely keep in touch. Thank you again for your interest.

LETTER 7-10 Thank You for Contact—General

It was a pleasure speaking with you on the phone last week.

I want to thank you for arranging for me to meet with Bill Stern on Monday, May 24, at 10:30 A.M. In preparation for this meeting, I have reviewed all the press releases posted on the website, and I am also reviewing the annual report that you kindly forwarded to me.

I am looking forward to meeting Mr. Stern and discovering more about Hyland, Kincaid, Stern.

Thank you again for your kind assistance.

CHAPTER 8

The Make Something Happen Letter

IT NEVER FAILS. You submit your resume, you ace the interview, and then you wait . . . and wait . . . and wait. Who knows why? Most likely, the firm hired another candidate without informing you (rude, but common). However, there is also the chance that the hiring process was interrupted because of budget cuts, a hiring freeze, or downsizing, or even because the company was put up for sale. Perhaps the decision makers are having difficulty choosing from among a strong field of candidates. Or perhaps the person responsible for hiring has simply taken a three-week vacation.

How to Jump-Start a Stalled Candidacy

Whatever the reason for the unnerving quiet, you should consider yourself a viable candidate until you hear otherwise. If you haven't heard anything, you haven't heard "no," so take advantage of the uncertainty. Return to the computer, and keep that motivation high. Try to get the hiring process moving in your direction. Writing and sending a well-planned Make Something Happen Letter demonstrates your eagerness to work for the person or the firm *and* your ability to follow through on an endeavor to completion—both of which are impressive qualifications to most employers.

The Make Something Happen Letter is aptly named, as its purpose is, quite literally, to make something happen: to rev the hiring engines; to represent yourself as a sterling candidate for the open position; to sway the decision maker's opinion away from your competitors and toward you. In writing this letter or e-mail, your *primary goal* is to promote yourself. Your *secondary goal* is to jump-start the hiring process. And with a little preparation, you can accomplish both simultaneously.

Before you begin to write, take a moment to reassess the situation. Be certain that you have not been rejected so graciously that you may have misunderstood. Be certain that you are a viable candidate, with relevant skills and experience; if you are irrefutably *un*qualified, there may be little point in pushing now. Most important, try to discern whether the person to whom you're writing will be receptive to your assertiveness.

If you determine that you are a reasonable candidate and that an active, aggressive step is called for, the "make something happen" letter can often do the trick. If you're unsure, but you figure that it's worth a shot, lessen the risk by matching the tone of voice you use in your e-mail to that of your reader or the position you seek. Many of the samples that follow in this chapter involve sales positions, for which assertiveness is a desired quality; the e-mails reflect this trait in the tone the writers adopt.

Step 1: Get to the Point

No two "make something happen" letters are the same. Each relates specifically to the position you're after, the organization you'll be a part of

---

RECRUITER'S TIP ⟩ **Resume Lost... and Found**

Not hearing anything after sending your resume or after interviewing may, indeed, mean that you haven't been selected.

Or, it could mean that the firm has:

- No system for responding.
- Actually lost your resume.
- Never received your resume.
- Added your resume to "the stack."
- Not completed interviewing.

So *write*! Make selection an active—not a passive—choice on the firm's part.

when you have been hired, the industry, the characters of those with whom you're dealing, and your own personality. Weigh each of these elements in your effort to create an appropriate opening line.

A conservative industry, for example, might dictate the use of a reserved, understated tone. Or, a bolder approach might be effective in shaking things up a bit. Writing to an interviewer who appears to be all suit and wing tips, who would never dress casually on Friday, might call for a completely different opening from one that you would use with a colleague you've known for years or someone working in a more relaxed environment, as technology or entertainment settings can be. You'll find examples of these and other openings in the samples that follow.

If your instinct has proved generally reliable in the past, you'll probably conjure up an opening that is clever, yet appropriate. If you're uncertain, adopt a more conservative approach. The bottom line, however, is to get to the point. Your opening should never require as much time to read as you have invested in planning it. Whether you're thanking your reader for a meeting, reminding him of who you are, providing additional information or references, or asking for the job, get to the point. Then, move along to Step 2.

Step 2: Make the Point

A quick opening will direct your reader to the body of your letter, in which you'll make your central point (or points) clearly and concisely. In virtually every case, your "make something happen" letters will be brief.

Say something new in the body of your letter. There's no justification for repeating points that you've already made during an interview or in a previous e-mail—evidently, they didn't work the first time. Instead, provide new information that is meaningful and beneficial to the reader. If appropriate, furnish additional references that might support your candidacy. Offer to spend more time with your prospective employer, particularly if you suspect that the decision maker is having trouble selecting from a field of strong candidates. Send a link to an article or blog post that is germane to a topic that was discussed during your meeting. Inform your reader of a relevant event that has occurred since you met, such as a goal you achieved, an important sale you netted, an award you earned, or a project you successfully completed.

If you genuinely can't come up with a single idea to add, try summarizing your qualifications in order to reinforce the fact that you meet all the employer's requirements.

Whatever your reason for writing, state it succinctly. Remember that you're writing to get the hiring process moving, not to bog it down further.

Optional Step 3: The Killer Close

As you review the sample letters that follow, you'll encounter a variety of different styles. The rule of thumb is this: the more forceful the letter, the more hard-hitting the close. From the direct, "Hire me," to the warm, polite, "I hope all is well with you and look forward to seeing you soon," each letter reflects the specifics of that writer's situation and the players involved.

The assessment of your own situation that you make before beginning to write should carry you through to your close, if you choose to include one. Continue with the same tone of voice you've used throughout the letter. Changing your tone now will make you sound insincere.

RECRUITER'S TIP ⟩ **Who Says There's No Free Lunch?**

If you're unemployed, you may need to get a bit creative.

If it's appropriate for your industry, offer to do the job on a trial basis, part-time, for a special salary arrangement or for free (with a time limit, of course, and a promise—in writing—to hire you should you meet their conditions).

Samples

LETTER 8-1 ▸ Make Something Happen—General

Our last discussion left me thoroughly convinced that I can produce dramatic results for your organization.

Count on my intelligence, experience, innate "people power," top-notch positioning, negotiation, and follow-up skills to bring in the steady stream of business you seek.

Hire someone with the know-how, the guts, and the goods to succeed. Hire someone who's as committed to performance as you are.

Hire me.

Strong opening.

Equally strong close.

To keep her name in front of the decision maker, this writer sends additional recommendations supporting her candidacy. Notice her tone of voice: positive, yet polite.

LETTER 8-2   Make Something Happen—Teacher

I had the pleasure of meeting with Marie Hammer last month regarding the opening in the Math Department at Habingdon High School. Because she indicated that you are a member of the selection team, I thought I would forward to you my most recent recommendations, which are attached.

In May of 20XX, I received my MA in Math Education from the University of Vermont, where I was fortunate to have been selected to assist Dr. Michael Gutfreund with his research on the visual acquisition of math skills. Since then, I have been teaching at Prescott South, and have thoroughly enjoyed my experience there.

Thank you for your time. I would consider it a privilege to meet with you in person!

Envisioning a tough selection choice, this candidate offers to meet again with the decision makers, and suggests an additional course of action that even the employer may not have considered. Notice the creative visual approach.

LETTER 8-3 ▸ Make Something Happen—General

Now that we've met several times, you know more about me. For instance, you know that...

I am loyal and reliable.

I am willing to take on any project.

I see things through to completion.

I help my coworkers whenever I can.

<u>I want very much to work for you!</u>

Now that your hiring deadline is approaching, perhaps I can help make your selection easier. Please feel free to call me in at any time for another meeting. I would be happy to meet with others on your staff or to complete a sample assignment for you.

I look forward to hearing from you.

LETTER 8-4 ▶ Make Something Happen—Sales

Unusual opener grabs attention.

No, I could not be more eager to join forces with you! Yes, as the new leader of your sales team, I will use and foster effective sales skills like this: <u>follow through until the deal is closed</u>.

That's why I'm writing to you again—to remind you of the uncommon benefits I will deliver as your Sales Manager:

- The advantage of <u>existing</u> profitable relationships with decision makers at top retailers in all major markets.

- Unusual strength in perceiving industry trends and challenges, and translating them into sales opportunities—well before others do.

- Proven ability to put these advantages to work for you from day one.

As you know, I am very eager to join your team. Please let me know if I can help you make your selection by providing any supplemental information or coming in for another interview. Feel free to call me at work or at home.

Instead of including them all on his resume, this jobhunter saved several additional accomplishments for just this purpose—to make something happen.

LETTER 8-5   Make Something Happen—Sales/Management

Since my eye-opening and mouth-watering visit to your headquarters (thank you again for your time!), during which my meeting with Paul Salamone was unexpectedly interrupted, I've been fortunate to have resumed that conversation yesterday.

As did the discussion that you and I had, my conversation with Mr. Salamone fanned my desire to be a strong and vital part of your sales team.

For evidence of the experience and maturity I can offer you, you have only to look at the outstanding results I've produced in a variety of marketplaces under a variety of market conditions. But should you seek greater confirmation, I have attached an overview of my accomplishments in both sales and management, which I also forwarded to Mr. Salamone.

I have no doubt that these successes are but a preview of what I can produce for you and your organization. I look forward to speaking with you soon.

LETTER 8-6   Make Something Happen—Travel—Sales

It was a pleasure meeting with you yesterday morning, and I thank you for your time.

Good reason
to write...
nice tie-in.

I thought you'd be interested in this article: http://blog.ted.com/20XX/06/13/post-2013-iran-election/, which I came across this morning, analyzing the public's reaction to the election of moderate Hassan Rouhani as successor to Mahmoud Ahmadinejad. It's the prospect of working with precisely this kind of challenge—where attitudes can change rapidly and dramatically—that is so <u>tremendously</u> exciting for me.

If you're looking for proven results within both the traveling private and public sectors, success within and outside of New York, the innovation it takes literally to find money, and someone who can hit the ground running—look no further. My expertise, interest, desire, and track record will fit perfectly.

I have always succeeded by finding or creating opportunities where others thought none existed; it's how I've become and remained top biller at Corporate Travel, Inc., and it's what I will do for you.

Let's make it happen!

The length of this letter is justified by the strong and in-depth support points the jobhunter has included to overcome her interviewer's concerns.

LETTER 8-7   Make Something Happen—Broadcast Sales

My meeting last week with you and Carol Keller has left me even more eager to work with you both, and the Sky Cable team. I am convinced that your needs and my talents are an ideal match. I take the liberty of sharing the reason for my confidence in order to reinforce our discussions!

When I joined WDEN, my list was by no means the largest at the station. I built it to the top-billing list and keep it there through concentrated effort and exceptional organizational skills, and by finding new and better ways to serve the customer—**as I will do for you.**

I provide consistent, thorough service to my clients. When my clients invest in the station, it's a direct result of the TRUST they have in me. Not only do I accurately book a large volume of orders, but I regularly monitor schedules to assure correct placement and rotations—which also limits discrepancies and ensures payment.

I serve as a valuable resource for my clients. Thanks to my strong research background, my sales technique goes well beyond selling numbers out of a rating book (at which I excel). To give clients and prospects more information and insight, I take advantage of qualitative marketing tools such as competitive data, online news, and trade sites.

Finally, clients get the benefit of my experience, which is broad and unique. Having been a Local Sales Manager, sold nationally, and worked for a major station group, I have sold a diverse range of products in diverse markets. This exposure has broadened my outlook and enables me to help my clients pinpoint target audiences by identifying appropriate vehicles on my station or through a combination of stations and cable networks to improve client efficiencies and our bottom line.

A cliché perhaps, but one I subscribe to, is that the key to success is to "work harder and be smarter"—both of which I want to do for you!

After meeting with the director of sales and the sales manager several times, this jobhunter wrote to both people to make something happen. Notice the link between this letter and the previous one.

LETTER 8-8 Make Something Happen—Broadcast Sales

I've attached a copy of a letter I sent to Anton Revinsky yesterday, which I want to make sure you see as well.

As I wrote to him, our meeting last week left me more convinced of the advantages that I can offer Sky Cable—and I wanted to reinforce these important benefits.

I am extremely eager to work with you, with the Sky Cable team, and in an environment where my talents can be applied to produce groundbreaking bottom-line results. Please let me know if there is anything else I can do to make this happen—or if you or Anton have any further questions or need additional information or references.

LETTER 8-9   Make Something Happen—Content Editor/Writer

In addition to my previously submitted resume, I thought this packet of writing samples, written for *The Online Business Journal*, would be useful.

Your job posting calls for a candidate who is experienced in transforming complex detail into engaging content. As my resume illustrates, I have in-depth experience in interpreting, organizing, and clearly conveying those essential elements that make a story sizzle. (In addition, I am skilled at ghostwriting, which is handy for composing speeches.) In the *Journal*'s "Insights" blog, I translate the technical jargon of business leaders into logical, straightforward content. Examples are attached.

Since our meeting last month, I have completed a short-term project working as editor and advocate for a foreign-born doctoral candidate. I framed his ideas into clear prose, and often clarified conceptual problems relating to his thesis.

I sincerely hope to hear from you soon.

Your make something happen letter can take unusual forms, as in this example.

LETTER 8-10   **Make Something Happen—General**

After her interview and after sending her follow-up e-mails, this executive knew that she was among the finalists for a job she very much wanted. To pivot the hiring decision in her direction, she sent her prospective employer this gift by messenger.

In Tiffany's signature blue box with its white ribbon, she placed a walnut shell, which she had previously emptied of its fruit.

Inside the shell, she put a small slip of paper, slightly bigger than the paper on which fortunes are printed in traditional fortune cookies. Along with her handwritten signature, the paper contained the following typewritten message:

> In a nutshell, I would love to work for you.
> *Ann Trip*

She got the job!

Here is another unique take on the gutsy approach.

LETTER 8-11   **Make Something Happen—Financial Services**

A jobhunter who was seeking a high-level position at a leading financial services corporation knew that he was a finalist. To keep his name squarely in the decision maker's mind, he sent an overnight express package containing a smaller box. In this box, he placed a length of adding machine tape. On the tape, he had typed the following message and signed it.

> **GREGORY ALLEN**
> (555) 987-6543
>
> BA, Finance
> MBA, Economics
> 14 Yrs. Experience
> Published E-zine Articles
> VP, Economists Society
> Panelist, Money Forum
> Exceptional Track Record
> + Superior
> Recommendations
>
> ---
>
> = Increased Profitability
> for USD Corporation
>
> Bottom Line: Let's make
> it happen!
>
> *Greg Allen*

LETTER 8-12 ▸ Make Something Happen—Sales

With your hiring deadline fast approaching, perhaps I can simplify this difficult decision with a brief review of what I can accomplish for you.

New Business Development: Like the 40 new customers I've brought in during the last six months alone.

Growth: Like the 20% increase in sales I achieved last year.

Leadership: Like the respect my team members have for me, as demonstrated in the letters of reference I've provided for you, the recommendations on my LinkedIn profile, and the mentoring program I created.

I have not concealed my excitement at the prospect of working with you because it's the same enthusiasm that I bring to my sales efforts, and to supporting my coworkers in their efforts.

Please let me know if there is anything else I can do to influence your decision in my favor.

LETTER 8-13 ▸ Make Something Happen—General

Super visual treatment.

Mediocrity
didn't take Fargo Manufacturing
to the heights it has achieved to date.

Mediocrity
won't put your bottom line at the top of the industry.

Mediocrity
is what you avoid when you hire the best.

Who is the best?

The answer is before you.

Here is an effective way to handle a familiar, frustrating scenario.

LETTER 8-14 **Make Something Happen—General—Phone Tag**

Since you and I are in the midst of "phone tag," I thought I would write you a quick note. It was a real pleasure meeting you several weeks ago, and discussing the exciting opportunities within Ladimor Worldwide.

You mentioned that it would make sense for me to speak with John Allen to learn more about the International Division. Given your busy schedule, I have taken the liberty of contacting him directly, and have scheduled an appointment for next week. I am looking forward to meeting him and will let you know the results of our session.

Very proactive!

Thank you again for your time.

Here is an excellent e-mail from a part-time worker who is anxious to transform her position into a full-time one.

LETTER 8-15   Make Something Happen—Consultant—
Part-Time/Full-Time

Working with you and your exceptional team over the past 16 months has been exceedingly rewarding, and for this I thank you.

My status as a consultant notwithstanding, you and your colleagues have welcomed me as a regular, valuable member of your team. You have given me the authority to supervise coworkers, create budgets, and represent the objectives of senior management in the successful execution of projects of my own design.

> She makes it hard to argue with success.

I am gratified to report that my efforts have produced authentic results: 52 new clients, $3.2 million in new sales, and a 9% reduction in overhead expenses. With the acquisition of such significant new business, the corporate culture is simultaneously rejuvenated, and the corporate image is reaffirmed.

Results such as these are precisely what I intended to achieve for you—and what I hope to continue bringing to the firm. I would welcome the opportunity to make my success a permanent contribution at the firm.

Let's get together to discuss this promising partnership. I'll call you shortly.

LETTER 8-16   Make Something Happen—General—
Create an Opportunity

Three weeks ago, we had the opportunity to meet and discuss the possibility of providing additional office support for your agents.

Since you were just beginning to explore this prospect at that time, I realize that it may be a while before you are ready to make a decision. For this reason, I am writing to restate my interest and to recap my qualifications.

My present position was a start-up position—one that was also new to the company. In this role, I began by immediately assessing tasks that needed to be fulfilled. I then created the position and my role to meet the goals of the individual representatives, and the corporation as a whole, most effectively. This required initiative, the ability to organize people and tasks, and the confidence to work in a new environment and quickly achieve rapport with the executives and staff.

<u>I can do the same for you.</u>

I am excited by the challenge of creating a new position. Allow me to use my expertise to make this position a meaningful, productive part of your organization.

I am available to meet again to answer any additional questions you may have.

LETTER 8-17 ▸ Make Something Happen—Special Education

I am extremely honored to be among the finalists for the position of Assistant Special Education Chairperson in District 43. Our meetings have convinced me that it would be a genuine pleasure to work with you and the members of your staff.

To assist you with what may be a difficult selection process, let me summarize the expertise I have acquired during my 18-year career in Special Ed:

- Diagnostic and prescriptive evaluations
- Case management
- Team facilitation
- Development of IEPs and individualized curricula
- Mainstreaming
- Staff training
- Parent counseling
- Child advocacy
- Coordination of therapeutic ancillary services
- Preparation of proposals for federal, state, and private grants

I gained this diverse experience working with developmentally disabled (including those at every level of the autism spectrum), emotionally handicapped, and multiply handicapped children from preschool age to age 21.

It would be a pleasure to bring to CSE-43 my familiarity and hands-on contributions in each of these vital areas. If there is any other information you require, please let me know. I would be happy to return for additional interviews at any time.

Thank you again for your time and consideration.

LETTER 8-18   Make Something Happen—Education

Since you've seen my CV, you know that I have been an educator for more than 11 years.

Since we've met several times, you know that I still retain the drive, energy, and commitment it takes to excite students in a subject that they find dull, at best—and irrelevant, at worst.

Since we've discussed my good fortune in receiving the State of Connecticut's "Outstanding Educator Award," you know that my abilities are well recognized, for which I am grateful.

So, if there is any uncertainty at all, please be assured **beyond a shadow of a doubt** that I am extremely eager to bring my talents and experience to bear on behalf of the students, families, faculty, and administration of my new home in South Helena.

I thank you once again for your time and candor.

> "Parallel construction" adds strength to the writer's message.

LETTER 8-19   Make Something Happen—General

You have been so generous with your time and attention during the past few weeks that I must express my gratitude.

Rarely have I enjoyed an interview process as thoroughly as I have yours. You and your staff have made me feel entirely welcome at American Home Services. There is no doubt in my mind that I will be able to fit into your organization and corporate culture at once—and begin contributing immediately to your reputation for service and your overall profitability.

If there is anything else I can do to demonstrate how ideal the match is between your needs and my strengths, please let me know. The opportunity to work closely with you is tremendously exciting.

Thanks again for your time and consideration.

With best regards,

LETTER 8-20   **Make Something Happen—Senior Management**

Killer opening.

30% reduction in overhead. 43% reduction in operating costs. 12% reduction in staff. 20% reduction in employee benefits expenses.

These are the savings I achieved for Morgan Engineering and the potential I offer to the Linder Organization.

Killer close.

Another day (without me)... another dollar (spent).

Sincerely,

Milton V. Childress

Additional Jobhunting Letters

EFFECTIVE NETWORKING PAYS off not only in your current job search, but in any searches you may undertake in the future, as well. For this reason, it's imperative that you treat with respect anyone with whom you have had contact during the jobhunt. You never know who may provide your next lead or job offer! So it pays to take a few minutes to acknowledge your interactions with those you encounter. If you don't, you can certainly predict who will *not* provide your next lead or job offer!

The Reference Request

Always get permission to use someone as a reference. In many cases, this may be done by telephone. But when you choose to write, make your e-mail or letter straightforward and to the point. Supply the person who will be serving as your reference with information on anyone who might be contacting him or her to discuss your qualifications. If you know who will be contacting your reference, say so; provide names, titles, and companies, and state the position for which you are interviewing. If you can't be specific, describe the *types* of positions for which you'll be interviewing. Always send your resume to the person who is serving as your reference—either with your request or afterwards. You'll find sample reference request letters later in this chapter.

The Meeting Confirmation

On some occasions, you may wish to confirm a meeting or an interview in writing. Such letters are always short, polite, and to the point. Reconfirm all pertinent details: date, time, location, with whom you'll be meeting, what you'll bring, what they'll bring, for what position you're interviewing, and so on. By all means, reconfirm your interest in the position or the company by making your letter sound enthusiastic. Samples follow.

(Note: If you're using your confirmation as an excuse to make a pre-meeting sales pitch to your interviewer or to provide additional information prior to a second meeting, you're really writing an ad response and resume cover letter or a follow-up letter; refer to the chapters that focus on these types of letters.)

The Job Acceptance

If you choose to write one, your acceptance letter should be short, precise, and to the point. In it, you can simply say yes to a job offer. Or you can confirm, in writing, the results of your jobhunting, interview, and negotiation efforts: the terms of your employment agreement. Remember that whatever you put in writing stays on the record, so be certain that your facts are accurate.

The Negotiation of an Offer

Typically, negotiating a job offer is handled in person or by phone, and often by a recruiter or placement agent. If you find that you must negotiate in writing, be clear and to the point. Justify your requests with support points that are important to the reader. Above all, remember that whatever you put in writing is on the record forever. Don't exaggerate, prefabricate, or make promises you can't keep.

The Offer Rejection

Whether or not you've turned down a job offer in person, you may wish to put it in writing as well. You may, for example, be asked to put your rejection in writing for the company's records, or you may wish to do so for your own records. (If, however, you're writing to maintain friendly relations so that you may be considered for future positions, this is a follow-up letter.) If the interview process was lengthy, you may wish to give a reason for your decision ("Although you had... , I chose to...."). Generally, there's no need to say where you've accepted an alternative job, especially if you've switched industries. If the person to whom you're writing has gone out of his or her way on your behalf, be sure to acknowledge his or her kindness.

The Letter of Resignation

Congratulations! Your hard work paid off with a job offer that you've accepted. Now comes the fun part: quitting your current job!

You've heard the advice of the experts, "Don't burn your bridges." They counsel against composing a scathing, biting attack on your old boss, your mean-spirited coworkers, the associate who sabotaged you, and the negative corporate culture. And they're right, because you never know where these people will land when they switch jobs—perhaps at the firm you've longed to work for all your life. Who knows? You might be asked to return and serve as their boss one day! (Isn't revenge sweet?)

So now is the time to write a professional, positive letter of resignation. You simply state that you are relinquishing your position and when. That is all you are required to do, although few people stop at that. The following samples demonstrate several alternative methods for resigning: the happy camper, the disgruntled (but professional) employee, and the one who "plays it close to the vest."

Choose your own style—just remember, whatever you put in writing remains on the record forever!

Samples

This jobhunter maintained the pleasant tone of voice she used in this letter in her subsequent thank you letter (see Letter 7-7).

LETTER 9-1 Reference Request—Student

After all you've done for me—as professor, advisor, and friend—do I dare ask for more? Well, I must, so here goes. Would you be willing to serve as a reference for me in my job search?

As you know, I'd like to join the training program of a financial services organization in the St. Louis area. In fact, I have already interviewed with three firms, each of which has asked me to provide references. With your permission, I will have the following people contact you:

1. John Brunswick, Loan Officer
   St. Louis Federal Bank
2. Muriel Howard, Vice President
   Credit Services
   Clayton Bank and Trust
3. Leslie Rubin, President
   South County Credit Union

Knowing how busy your schedule is at this time of year, I will call your office next Wednesday during the late afternoon to see whether you're able to speak with these people.

I thank you in advance for your time and help.

LETTER 9-2 Reference Request

I hope this letter finds you well and prosperous. During my tenure at Burke Enterprises, your insistence on premier product innovations was legendary. Since then, I have kept abreast of Burke's impressive growth, so I know that your admonitions are still being heeded.

As you may recall, I left Burke when my wife's firm sent her to California to open a West Coast division. After two years with the government, I am now in the process of continuing my career in product development, and would consider it an honor to add your name to the top of my list of references.

With your approval, I will authorize representatives of firms with which I am in the final stages of the selection process to contact you. I have enclosed an updated resume with this letter to remind you of my qualifications—and I will call you shortly to see whether you might be willing to assist me. If so, I will provide you, *in advance*, with the names of those who may be in touch with you.

I was grateful for your thoughtfulness and support when I was part of the Burke team, and I am equally grateful now for your help.

LETTER 9-3 Meeting Confirmation

I am looking forward to meeting you on January 12, 20XX, at 3:00 P.M. at the Pleasantville Hyatt to discuss the instructional design position in your East Coast office.

I feel certain that my training and experience will prove valuable to you, and I am eager to provide you with details on my background.

LETTER 9-4 ▸ Acceptance of Job Offer

It is with great pleasure that I accept your offer to serve as an Instructional Designer for your East Coast office. I look forward to joining HealthCom beginning on March 1, 20XX, with a starting salary of $65,000 per year.

I am especially eager to work with Dawn Sinclair in your new Professional Development Unit.

Thank you for your assistance and consideration.

This letter and the one that follows differ only slightly—but on the rare occasions that job negotiations are put in writing, details like these are of key importance.

LETTER 9-5 ▸ Negotiation of Job Offer—Publishing

You've certainly built an exceptional editorial team over the years, and your offer to join it is enormously gratifying.

As you know, I am very eager to accept this honor. I look forward to bringing my contacts and authors to Brockridge Publishing. Because these relationships are ones that I've nurtured for more than 10 years, they're naturally of great value to me—and to you. The profit potential that they represent is substantial. I feel it is reasonable and fair to adhere to my request for a 10% stake in the profits these properties generate.

Harold, in light of the many benefits of our joining forces, this detail seems minor. It is, however, of great importance to me. Let's agree on this right away, and launch our promising partnership!

I look forward to hearing from you.

LETTER 9-6 ▶ Negotiation of Job Offer—Publishing

You've certainly built an exceptional editorial team over the years, and your offer to join it is enormously gratifying.

As you know, I am very eager to accept this honor. I look forward to bringing my contacts and authors to Brockridge Publishing. Because these relationships are ones that I've nurtured for more than 10 years, they're naturally of great value to me—and to you. The profit potential that they represent is substantial. I feel it is reasonable to request a share in the profits that these properties generate. Let's agree on a specific percentage right away, and launch our promising partnership!

I look forward to hearing from you.

LETTER 9-7 ▶ Rejection of Job Offer

Thank you very much for offering me the position of Instructional Designer for your East Coast office. Unfortunately, I am unable to join HealthCom's staff at this time because I have just accepted another firm's offer.

I am very grateful to you for your assistance during the interview process, and I genuinely appreciate your consideration.

LETTER 9-8 ▶ Rejection of Job Offer

I am writing to withdraw my name from consideration for the position of Executive Administrative Assistant with your firm, as I have accepted an offer from another company.

However, I thank you sincerely for your time and candor in describing both the position and the corporate culture. You were most kind, and I appreciate the encouragement you offered me.

With best wishes for your continued success,

This letter is short, sweet, and to the point—very professional!

LETTER 9-9 **Resignation Letter**

With this letter, I hereby submit my resignation from Burger Products International, effective Friday, June 4, 20XX, to further my career in facilities management.

At your convenience, I will be glad to discuss the reassignment of my work to others.

I wish you good luck and continued success.

This writer reminds her boss of the productive changes she's implemented. Nice touch!

LETTER 9-10 **Resignation Letter**

I am writing to inform you that I will be resigning my responsibilities as Comptroller effective March 1, 20XX.

I realize that selecting and introducing a new Comptroller may be difficult, and I will do whatever I can to make this transition a smooth one. In large part, the streamlined accounting and recordkeeping practices I developed during the last four years will help a new Comptroller master our systems, database, and payroll quickly.

I am pleased to have had the opportunity to work with Technix. I wish you continued success and growth.

The cleverly worded opening paragraph may leave the reader wondering what this writer's opinion of the company really is—but its clever wording won't endanger the writer's reputation or future.

LETTER 9-11   Resignation Letter

Effective November 30, I am resigning from my job as Media Director at Mercury Advertising. My decision to leave is both personal and professional, and does not reflect a change in my opinion of the company.

Donna Frey has performed admirably as my assistant, and is well equipped to assume my responsibilities at once. If you prefer to look outside the company to replace me, I will be happy to assist in the search between now and the end of the month.

Thank you for your continued confidence in me throughout the past two years.

CHAPTER 10

Killer Resources

IF YOU'VE MADE it this far, the hard part is done. You've identified your strengths, determined what benefits they offer your next employer, and fashioned them into sentences and paragraphs that you can use in your jobhunting letters, e-mails, and notes. You've written attention-grabbing openings and action-oriented closings. You're ready to send your own killer cover letters. Before you hit Send, though, take a few minutes to be certain that you've thought of everything.

The following pages will help ensure that your letters are really as strong as they possibly can be.

First, scan the list of words and phrases to avoid. If your letter is replete with jargon, your message may not get through as clearly as it should.

Then, run down the Cover Letter Checklist to help ensure that you've included everything correctly and that you are, indeed, ready to send your Killer Cover Letters on their way.

The most valuable of all talents is that of never using two words when one will do.

—THOMAS JEFFERSON

Words and Phrases to Avoid

Avoid	Use Instead
additionally	in addition
along the lines of	like
alot	a lot
alright	all right
answer in the affirmative	say yes
arrived at the conclusion that	concluded
as per	I find or according to
as stated above	from these facts or as I have shown
at a later date	later
at the present time	now
at the present writing	now
at the time of three in the afternoon	at 3:00 P.M.
at this point in time	now
attached hereto	attached
attached herein	attached
attached please find	attached is or attached you'll find or I enclose
awaiting the favor of a response	please let me know
beg to inform you	inform you
came at a time when	came when
city of New Orleans	New Orleans
close to the point of	close to
concerning the matter of	concerning or about
due to the fact that	because
enclosed herewith	enclosed
enclosed please find	enclosed is or enclosed you'll find or I enclose
fewer in number	fewer or less

file away	file
for the purpose	for or to
for the reason that	because
for your information	(delete entirely)
in accordance with your request	as you requested
in respect to the matter of	about or regarding
in the amount of	for
in the area of	about
in the field of accounting	in accounting
in the near future	soon or shortly
in the neighborhood of	about
in this day and age	now or today
inasmuch as	since
irregardless	regardless
is at this time	is
most unique	unique
my personal opinion	my opinion
myriad of	myriad
of the fact that	(delete entirely)
on the grounds that	because
on the occasion of	when (or state the occasion)
prior to	before
prolong the duration	prolong
quality	high quality or low quality, superior quality or poor quality
shows a preference for	prefers
subsequent to	after
that is the reason why	that is why
the reason is due to	because
the undersigned	I
utilize	use

with reference to	about
with regard to	about or regarding
with respect to	about
without further delay	now or immediately

Cover Letter Checklist

_____ Have you proofread your letter both before *and after* using spell-check? (Remember, your computer won't catch an error such as "thin" instead of "this.")

_____ Does your letter look visually appealing?

_____ If your letter is skimmed, will your reader be impressed with the key points?

_____ Will your reader know the ad or job posting to which you're responding? The position in which you're interested?

_____ Will your opening make the reader want to read on?

_____ Does the body of your letter support your opening?

_____ Is your letter honest?

_____ Is your tone of voice conversational, not stuffy?

_____ Have you avoided repeating, word for word, many of the details that appear on your resume?

_____ Have you summarized your experience and education?

_____ Have you described your strengths from your reader's point of view? ("What this means for you is....")

_____ Did you provide necessary background information in cases where a reader or recruiter is unfamiliar with you or your area of specialty?

_____ Have you used any terminology that might be unfamiliar to your reader? Can you simplify it? If not, have you defined it clearly?

_____ Have you told your reader what you will do to follow up?

_____ Did you supply any and all information your reader will need to contact you or comply with your request for help?

The Online Jobhunter's Checklist

Now you're ready to begin the process that will ultimately lead to your landing the job you want! To help speed your search, this checklist will remind you of all the information and tips included in this book. Here is your step-by-step guide through the process of executing all the elements of an effective job search. Good luck!

■ **Commit!** Decide to spend a set amount of time each day focusing on your search. For some people, that may be two to three hours each day; for others, it could be two hours twice a day. If it helps, identify specific hours, such as 8:30 to 10:30 A.M. each weekday. Although it may not seem like much time, if you are disciplined about using it wisely and consistently, it can add up to a concerted effort and a significant investment on your part—*precisely what is required to speed your search to an effective conclusion.*

How will you spend your time? Refining your resume and cover letters. Networking online, on the phone, and in person at conferences, events, gatherings, and meetings. Expanding your knowledge and skills through coursework, professional development, and volunteer work. Remember to stay active. Sitting at the computer all day is not healthy either physically or emotionally, and it can be frustrating.

■ **Explore!** If you are new to the job search, investigate some of the many websites that offer advice—you can use this link to find more websites in the downloadable content that accompanies this book: http://www.mhprofessional.com/mediacenter. You're bound to discover promising new ideas and approaches, step-by-step instructions, guidance, and helpful hints—as well as pitfalls to avoid—that will help you conduct an effective search. As you navigate from site to site, it's likely that you'll be redirected quite a bit, making it tough to keep track of valuable sites to which you'd like to return. So try right-clicking on a link, which gives you the option of opening it in a new tab, keeping each site open for easy return. You can also bookmark or save as "Favorites" the sites that you find especially useful and want to revisit from time to time.

■ **Search!** Decide what type of positions you want to apply for, then make a note of the various job titles associated with the positions that interest you. This list will help you search for openings that appeal to you. If you find that you're not getting the results you wish, experiment with different words or combinations. For example, you might begin with "Customer Service," only to encounter an unmanageable number of openings. In that case, you can narrow your search by trying "Retail Customer Service," "Online Customer Support," "Bank Customer Service," or even "Seattle Bank Customer Service."

■ **Prepare!** Have your resumes and cover letters ready to upload for online applications. After writing, proofing, and spell-checking them, then proofing them again, be sure you have named each file accurately and appropriately. Not only will you want easy access to it, but the document titles should be useful to your readers, as well. A nurse might have one version of a resume for applying to hospitals titled "CDiaz Hospital R.N. Resume" and another tailored for schools, which might be named "CDiaz School Nurse Resume." The same would hold true for the accompanying cover letters.

■ **Reach out to References!** Don't wait until the last minute to prepare your professional references. They will surely be requested by a recruiter, hiring manager, or interviewer or as part of the online application process. Identify several people for whom or with whom you've worked; obviously you'll want to choose those you can count on to speak well of you. Employers typically ask for three references, but you should identify more in case anyone declines or is unavailable at the moment his or her support is needed.

Then, write to each of these people, explaining what type of position you're seeking and what your timing is; include a copy of your resume. (You'll find sample letters in Chapter 9.) This will remind them of your accomplishments, reassure them that you are worth recommending, and facilitate access to it when they are contacted. Once you have heard back that they are willing to serve as references, an immediate thank you note is in order. Then, you should be in touch again when a connection is imminent; your references will appreciate knowing who will be calling or writing and what company or organization that individual represents. For the person who kindly agreed to serve as your reference, an unexpected call is not the ideal way to launch a discussion extolling your professionalism!

■ **Sign Up!** To take advantage of jobhunting, networking, and social websites that may provide assistance, you'll need to register and/or open an account on those sites you determine to be of value. To register, you'll need a professional e-mail address and a password, so be prepared. If you don't already have one, secure an e-mail address with your name in some form and a password that includes an uppercase letter, a symbol, and a number in case the site requires it. Of course, you will need to make a note of these somewhere so you don't forget them.

■ **Go Social!** Your online footprint is one source of information that recruiters and hiring managers will use to form an impression of you, so if you don't have an online profile, create one. If you do, check that it's current and professional. You should check regularly, and update if warranted, the sites on which recruiters can find you to be sure you're presenting an appropriate image. You can add to your profile any volunteer activities in which you've been engaged. Also remember to check and correct privacy settings on social media and networking sites, as they do change, often with little notice. (See "Manage Your Online Profile" in Chapter 1.)

■ **Organize!** To track applications, responses, interviews, conversations, contact info, connections, follow-up, correspondence, references, and more, you'll need to be organized. So create, adopt, or sign up for a system that matches your personality and style. You can create an Excel spreadsheet on your computer or a binder for your bookshelf that you fill with printouts. Or, you can use an online search management tool like JibberJobber. Choose what works for you, and use it regularly. Don't let a surprise call from a potential employer catch you unprepared!

■ **Network!** Now you're ready to start alerting friends, family, and colleagues that you are in the market for a job. Since networking is essential to identifying openings and reaching key decision makers, you simply can't afford to avoid this important step in your search. It is the *number one most effective way to find the position you desire.* Most jobhunters maintain an active presence on LinkedIn as well as on sites that target their specific industries or talents. Some employers even offer financial incentives for referred candidates who are hired, so you and your connections can both benefit. The amount and value of the information and contacts you'll gain through networking are impossible to quantify, so get connected and stay connected. The more you network, the more quickly you'll land the interviews that will lead to your next job. (Review the information on networking in Chapter 1 and all of Chapter 4.)

■ **Apply!** Now that you've created a solid foundation for your search, you're ready to start applying for jobs. Start looking for appropriate positions on one or more of the major job boards like Monster, TheLadders, or CareerBuilder. (Use this link to find more websites in the downloadable content that accompanies this book: http://www.mhprofessional .com/mediacenter.) You might also look on aggregate boards such as Indeed.com as well as relevant niche sites such as bankjobs.com, idealist .org, or diversity.jobs.careercast.com. Try to resist the temptation to apply (because it's so easy) for those jobs for which you truly are not qualified; after all, would you want your ideal qualifications overlooked because a hiring manager was inundated with too many applications to handle?

■ **Target!** If you know an industry or a company where you would like to work, then add that to your search and monitor that specific website for job opportunities. Find someone who works there (through your networking) who can act as a gatekeeper for you.

■ **Follow Up!** A jobhunter who plays on Facebook all day and uploads resumes for dozens of jobs is not likely to get very far, very fast. An effective search is about staying in touch with contacts, references, recruiters, hiring managers, interviewers, decision makers, potential employers, and anyone else who is in a position to help you. The suggestions and sample letters and e-mails in this book make it incredibly easy to send thank you and follow-up notes, make something happen letters, and more. So there's no excuse not to stay connected. (You'll find plenty of samples in Chapters 6, 7, and 8.) The more you write, the more you'll stay on people's "radar" and the faster your search will end successfully.

■ **Repeat!** Going through most of these steps again and again will ensure that you are conducting a thorough search. Because you will, either soon or eventually....

■ **Celebrate!** You've worked hard and landed the job you want, so now you've earned a celebration. Congratulations!

Index of Letters That Address Specific Issues

MANY OF THE letters in this book and in the downloadable content address specific issues that are of concern in today's jobhunting environment. To help you locate ways in which you might handle such situations, many of the letters throughout the book are labeled according to the issue they address. Such letters are also listed below for quick reference. (Letter 3-3, for example, refers to Chapter 3, Letter 3.)

For example, if you are returning to work after an absence, check the letters listed under "Workforce Return." If you are switching fields, refer to the letters listed under "Career Change." Graduating seniors and recent MBAs, be sure to review those listed under "Entry Level" and "Student" for ideas to adapt and use in your own letters.

Issue	Chapter and Letter Number
Career Change	4-4, 4-7, 4-8, 4-12, 5-20, 5-24, 5-27, 5-37, 5-44, 5-59, 5-71, 5-88, 5-89, 5-109
Confidentiality	5-49, 5-52, 5-58, 5-82, 5-101, 5-114
Entry Level	5-9, 5-12, 5-13, 5-14, 5-15, 5-16, 5-17, 5-20, 5-21, 7-6, 7-7, 9-1
International	5-10, 5-61, 7-1
Jobhopper	5-11, 5-46

Index of Letters by Industry and Job Title

ALL THE LETTERS and e-mails in this book and in the downloadable content are listed below by industry. (Letter 4-30, for example, refers to Chapter 4, Letter 30.) Jobs that fall under more than one category are listed under each grouping that may apply. For example, an Insurance Sales cover letter is listed under both "Financial Services" and "Sales."

Most important, don't limit yourself by reading only letters dealing with a specific job. Take the time to skim many of the letters in this book. Since your letters should not repeat what's on your resume, cover letters written by jobhunters in fields unrelated to yours can contain ideas that you can easily adapt for use in your own letters.

Alphabetical Listing of Letters

About the Authors

Sandra Podesta For more than 20 years, Sandra Podesta has used her writing talents to convince people to make decisions and act on them. Within the corporate environment, she has served at Fortune 500 companies as Product Manager, Creative Director, and Marketing Director. On the advertising agency side, she's lent her talents to both creative and account management teams. Sharing her communications strategies and experience, she delivers onsite and online training to equip professionals at every level to enhance productivity and increase profitability, sales teams to generate higher revenues, and nonprofit organizations to raise funds more effectively.

Entrepreneurs and business owners also appreciate TheLetterStore. com, Ms. Podesta's online e-commerce site, where they discover a variety of professionally written business letters that they can download, sign, and send immediately. In today's tough labor market, she guides and motivates jobhunters through online ResumeRoom.com resume and interview prep private sessions.

Andrea Paxton As a recruiter and human resources executive, Andrea Paxton has worked extensively with every phase of the interview, selection, hiring, and training processes. She has directed the recruiting efforts of global organizations and Fortune 500 companies, including AIG, John Hancock Financial Services, and Chase (now JPMorgan Chase), as well as designing and launching first-time recruitment programs for smaller regional firms.

A recognized innovator in her field, Ms. Paxton pioneered the use of traditional and nontraditional resources and is an expert in work-flow design, internal and external problem resolution, and mediation. She designed, implemented, and administered a highly selective and effective management training program for undergraduate and graduate candidates and has spoken at industry events including the NAACP Career Convention at the New York Coliseum.

Ms. Paxton frequently counsels jobhunters who are undergoing a career switch, a challenge that she successfully navigated herself when she became a licensed Life and Health Insurance Agent. She earned her bachelor of science in family and consumer studies and is a graduate of LIMRA's Agency Management Training Council, the industry's premier skill development program for field managers that enhances management skills in the critical areas of planning, recruiting, selection, training, and performance management.